4E573

WRESTLING WITH CHRIST

WRESTLING
WITH CHRIST

LUIGI SANTUCCI

TRANSLATED FROM THE ITALIAN BY
Bernard Wall

COLLINS
ST JAMES'S PLACE, LONDON,
1972

First published in Italy
in 1969 under the title
Volete Andarvene Anche Voi?

ISBN 0 00 215913 9

Set in Monotype Garamond.
Made and Printed in Great Britain by
William Collins Sons & Co Ltd Glasgow.

For my children

If Jesus had not lived,
then our life would be meaningless,
in spite of all the other people
whom we know and honour and love.

Dietrich Bonhoeffer

CONTENTS

Translator's Note   11

Author's Foreword   13

THE NATIVITY

The person who interests us   19

A down-at-heel gentleman   20

Days and nights   21

Dreams   22

Good-bye, Joseph   23

You'll call him Jesus   23

The pact   25

An eyeless monster   25

About good people and others   26

The first procession   27

The kick of joy   28

Conversation at 'Ain Karim   28

As in a valley   31

How many were there?   32

The second procession   32

Better that way   33

The end of dreams   34

Space and time   35

Twelve words   36

Naked and mad   37

The saints of gold   38

The deal   39

Those at the appointment   40

Joy and sorrow   41

Chorus of the innocents   42

A blank page   43

Those thirty years   44

Nazarene and Christ   46

A divine caprice   47

Why have you done this to us?   48

Straightaway   50

7

CONTENTS

THE MIRACLES
So that you'll believe . . .   54
The hour   57
His home   59
He was asleep in the stern   60
Fishes and men   61
A ghost   62
Peter, a man like me   63
Five and two make a hundred thousand   66
God's anger   67
The sick in public places   69
The theft   70
The miracles on the sabbath   72
The withered hand   72
Without a man   74
This isn't what we want   75
Who's going home?   77
A crossroads   78
An obstinate man   79
A little saliva   81
The masterpiece   82
If you want to . . .   84
A missed appointment   84
The other incarnation   89
Face to face   89
A father, a mother and a grain of seed   91
The word under the roof   93
Beata dormitio   94
Two superfluous words   96
Death is a flute   98
The friend behind the stone   100
The gift to the three   104

THE PARABLES
We didn't dance   107
Friends and enemies   108
Like an overturned cart   119

HUMAN ENCOUNTERS
How on earth?   125

CONTENTS

What more should I do?   127
The comeback   130
Jesus' honey   131
Another thirst   132
Flesh and stones   134
Two alabaster vases   136
The big throng   139
All with him   140

THE CITY
The exile   144
When?   146
Carnival at Jerusalem   149

THE PASSION
As long as we can stand it   152
From below   153
The hiding-place   155
One of us   158
The long good-bye   163
Silence   166
Sleep   168
Without wings or trumpet   170
The first wound   170
Ninepins   172
The sword and the caress   173
The cheek   174
Two turbans   175
Behind the bandage   177
The sleepwalker   178
Pontius Pilate's diary for posterity   180
A brilliant plan   183
Ecce Homo   184
Continuation of Pilate's diary   185
Red throats   186
Pilate's diary: conclusion   187
Insects   188
The orchestra   190
The blind ox   191

9

CONTENTS

The third hour   193
Those few words   195
The miracle he didn't want to perform   196
Today   198
Another paradise   200
Three hours of darkness   201
The glass of water you give . . .   203
Hands   204
The joyful dead   204
Shadows and scents   205

RESURRECTION AND ASCENSION

The two lovers   207
Why to me?   210
The race   212
We don't believe it   213
Touching, eating   215
The finger   215
The last picnic   216
The alphabet   217
Don't look up at the sky   219

TRANSLATOR'S NOTE

Usually a translator can't be identified with the book he translates. It's a problem like music. A pianist may prefer Mozart to Chopin, but this doesn't mean that he won't do his utmost to play Chopin. I hope readers will forgive me if I give this over-ambitious example. But in this book Signor Santucci raises a human problem very near to many of us.

The problem is that Jesus, called the Christ, is as mysterious as the existence of the universe itself. The mystery has been veiled by established conventions in society, clichés in language, and the behaviour of many people in our civilization who have dared to call themselves 'Christian'. I was brought up in the same traditions as Signor Santucci, and when I first read his book I thought he had embarked on an impossible task. How could any writer now describe Jesus Christ? How could he get beneath the encrustations of dead phrases (and memories) and approach the strangest person who has ever existed? How avoid getting embogged in so many centuries of book-learning, criticism and counter-criticism?

Then, as I thought over the matter further, I came to the same conclusion as my friend Giancarlo Vigorelli who wrote that Signor Santucci had 'pulled it off'. I thought that the book might have something in it that would appeal to many people in a plural society, agnostic, Catholic, Protestant or atheist. It occurred to me that if we lived on another planet, the wild story of Jesus wouldn't seem to us a cliché – we would be fascinated by it. Just as I find the accounts of the mystics of Islam (so like those of our own mystics in Spain) somehow renewing and fascinating. Signor Santucci is in the same jam as I am.

Perhaps some readers will be reminded of the poetic approach to love and the universe of a writer like Ignazio Silone. In our lay world, so I have found, laymen often say more to laymen about the question-marks of religion than do the disputations of theologians who, at times, seem to swallow a camel and then have subtle and abstract arguments about the needle. The contemplation of great painting, with which Signor Santucci is manifestly familiar, is a consoling part of 'Christian' culture. The approach may seem naïf to some but the wrestling is anything but arid or just 'literary', and the author is aware, as he shows time and time again, of the many sophisticated explanations of our existence in modern societies. His book reflects a not uncommon experience and could be helpful at a time when the gulf between clerical tastes and feelings and those of educated lay persons seems hardly to be narrowing.

What is essential is that readers shouldn't think of this poetic novel as a 'life of Christ'. It consists of a meditation on the universe, on us, on the challenge and response to extraordinary 'events' which happened 2,000 years ago and which influenced our uncontrollable history – us – more than anything else. The Greco-Roman world may bewitch us like a siren song. But it lacked one thing – pity or compassion.

Signor Santucci was born in Milan in 1918. He published his first novel, one of light humour, in 1947. In 1962 he stopped teaching in a *liceo* or *lycée* and has since written a number of books, at least one of which has won a literary prize. English-speaking readers may find some of his expressions strange; for instance his attitude to miracles, to the Madonna and, above all, to women (including whores) and children. Such things form part of the enormous contribution of the Italians to our civilization whether in Tuscan or Venetian art, or in writing.

I've taken some liberties with his style. Poetic Italian is a complicated language and where it differs from English most of all is in syntax. I've also taken some liberties with translations from the Gospels. I've attempted to translate the challenging statements made into the language we talk – as Signor Santucci wrote them in his mother tongue.

BERNARD WALL

FOREWORD

When, on the evening of a day of bitter humiliations and mass desertions, Jesus asked his companions, 'Do you want to go away too?' Peter answered with a phrase whose meaning depends on the emphasis with which it was said – was it fervent conviction or sudden misgiving? 'Lord, where should we go?' he said, 'only you have the words of eternal life.' Christ's question combined a vigorous challenge with a touching and ironical lack of coercion, and it occurs to us all at one time or another: 'Aren't you satisfied with me? Do I have an oppressive effect on you? Am I cheating you in some way?' – and the best we can do then is to make the sincerest answer we can, both to ourselves and to him.

But I feel there's a preliminary point. Before we decide whether to go or stay we need to re-examine the reality, in other words the life, of that man. Though he still remains a mystery, this is essential if we're to come to grips with him and question both him and ourselves.

This story of Christ (as it throws light on my own story and is an opportunity for a biography of myself and many others like me) is born of two moods of soul and has two sides. One glows with a faith in which Christ is enjoyed as a happy possession, a consoler and an answer; the other is marked by problems or even the abyss of despair. So this book, which I have put together over many and varied years, contains the Christian certainties and enthusiasms of some of my hours, and the weeds of anguish and doubt of others. Wheat and tares, as it is written, in the open field of life.

The whole narrative is taken from the Gospels. It follows their shape literally without any attempt to evaluate them historically or indulge in biblical criticism. The 'possessed' are accepted in accord with the views held in gospel times, not as victims of some neurotic illness or advanced psychosis. And Satan and the angels aren't treated as abstractions or allegories of the unconscious but behave as responsible

13

personified beings just as they do in the Gospels. Is it possible to write the story of Christ in such a non-critical way? Or, at a time when theology has leapt forward like the exploration of space, am I expressing some lunatic fringe? I haven't worried about that. *Ad extra* I've left forms and figures as the Gospels present them. But *ab intra* I've tried wherever possible to make the theological mystery credible to our thoughts and human experiences – that is, *to work for faith*. So, for instance, in treating the resurrection I felt it wasn't absurd but more widely acceptable (as I explain in the relevant section) that Christ should have risen through a sort of autochthonous act, under the supreme impulse of love for others and the impossibility of abandoning them. Or again, I saw the redemption of the woman taken in adultery and the guarantee that she would 'sin no more' in terms of the superiority of Christ's unique powers of seduction over the allurements of other men.

As for my 'technique', I couldn't see any way of writing the life of Christ except by constantly changing my angle. Thus on some pages I've dared to treat Christ autobiographically and let him make his own 'confession'; on others I've allowed myself to 'spy' into his human life and feelings, as well as into those of the people most closely involved in his story, from Mary to Satan, and from the apostles to Pilate. While I was doing this, that is to say while I was performing these indiscreet manipulations and subjectivizations, I realized that the figure of the Redeemer never lost its sacred aspect. This verified his super-humanity in my eyes and hence I felt I was writing a real *history*, an authentic biography of him.

Sometimes I've described his life as if I were a physical witness – now from within him, now from within myself. I've made so bold as to choose every possible way of telling this story and have adopted the exhaustive pluralism and co-existence of different planes from which contemporary story-telling seems unable to escape (and this can be found in the way the Gospels themselves are written). The use of psychology, theatrical dialogue, monologues of a *nature morte* type, sur-realistic distortions, elaborations, and commentary based

14

on my own life – all seemed to help to make Christ's figure explode to the maximum. In this way his life stands above hagiography and the narration of facts; it tends to become a *summa* of human arguments and passions. In the last analysis perhaps no more than a huge metaphor of our feelings and of the sense of the eternal.

I worked on this Christological 'test' during the years when both the secular and the religious worlds were in upheaval, and that guaranteed and fostered two things: freedom and faith. As I went over and over Christ's actions and what he said on earth I got a clearer grasp of why theology today is galloping forward and why it's no use trying to hold it back. It is right and 'Christian' that it should blow where it wants to blow, and the judgment we make on it has to be brought back to Christ, to the person who never repressed a free, generous and violent search for God – '*The hour has come when you won't worship the Father either on this mountain or in Jerusalem*'; '*the hour has come and this is it when the real worshippers will worship the Father in spirit and in truth.*' As for faith, rather than give it *to* me he has commanded it *of* me, and with almost passionate threats. He has taught me to look for it, discover it and love it more than my life. The reproach he makes to us is bludgeoning and unequivocal: 'Why don't you believe?'

After travelling with Christ through several hundred pages I am left with the conviction that if faith is everything then Christ himself is the key to the continuation or evaporation of faith on earth. But in a tortured way I also know that this faith can no longer be, either for me or for anyone else, the proverbial faith of the Breton peasant. This type of faith is dead; perhaps God does not want it any more, even though he told us to be as simple as little children. And so it is that this mysterious and contradictory fact of faith – balanced between orgies of research and holy simplicity – seems the most elusive and unpreachable thing, the thing which has most abandoned the world and by which the world wants to remain abandoned.

I must confess that when writing these pages I sometimes

had the impression of being a last-ditcher guarding a bridge for a defeated army that has long been in retreat. The world around me had its back turned towards me as if in centrifugal flight from the man whose story I was telling; and it seemed to me that this inevitably involved giving the lie to Christ and making any history of him null and void. But on other, more frequent, occasions I felt that in its existence – even in the hopelessness of its existence as I saw it – my world was not in opposition to Christ, nor did it mock him, nor did it forget him. Indeed, despite every apparent contradiction, I felt a mingled Christ-world to be true; and true and potent the words of Dietrich Bonhoeffer: 'The world has need of Christ *and nothing less. Christ died for the world and Christ is Christ only in the world.*'

I was in the world and thus perhaps was able to understand a little about Christ and dare to write about him. But what finally emerged in black and white can't really be called a life of Christ. It would be better to call it an attempt at a long and difficult prayer, an inconclusive struggle. As I accompanied Christ, not as an apologist or hagiographer but only as a man accustomed to using words, he became, as I said, a gigantic metaphor of our feelings. So it is possible that this book only presents him in a poetic dimension. But I personally cannot rule out that Christ's force, and the triumph of his journey within mankind, may lie in the last analysis in his *omnipotence* as a poet.

Whether we believe in him as incarnate Word or not, there lies in every man confronting Christ, in the very impact of his name, a sort of concealed fanaticism; his power of subjugating us prevails over everyone else's with a maximum of gentleness and violence. I suspect that everyone, of any faith or none, is inclined to say with the people of Jerusalem, 'No one has ever spoken like this man'. Dostoevsky expressed this heady seduction in his famous paradox: 'If I had to choose between Christ and the truth, it's Christ I would choose.' As for me, at this precise point in my life and the life of the world, the fascination and yoke of Christ are summed up in that little-known phrase, discovered as something new in the depths of the gospel: 'Do you want to go away too?'

Some will go, some will stay. The important thing (and I would wish it for my readers as much as for myself) is that if we make Peter's answer our own – and *stay* – our choice shouldn't be the product of habit, cowardice or fear: 'Where should we go?' If it is true that Christ alone has the words of eternal life, the choice of staying with him must not sound dispirited and lifeless – like that of someone choosing to surrender when encircled and with no way out: it must be grateful and liberating, like the answer of one who – when everything seems to be sinking in a storm – knows that henceforth he will experience no despair or loneliness. But this, too, depends on the protagonist of my story. For at table one evening he said, 'Without me you can do nothing.'

L.S.

THE NATIVITY

He dwelt among us.

THE PERSON WHO INTERESTS US

Abraham begot Isaac, Isaac begot Jacob; Jacob begot Judah and his brothers. Judah begot Phares and Zara out of Thamar . . .

Begot . . . begot . . . begot . . . It sounds like some arid catalogue and yet it is the gospel. Matthew is telling an extraordinary tale and is already pushing on to Christ. The written history of Jesus thus begins with outlandish names. *Naasson begot Salmon; Salmon begot Boaz out of Rachab; Boaz begot Obed out of Ruth; Obed begot Jesse; Jesse begot King David.* These men last as long as it takes to pronounce the syllables of their names, all coagulated in the word and act of begetting which Matthew's prose makes seem headlong.

King David begot Solomon out of the wife of Uriah; Solomon begot Rehoboam; Rehoboam begot Abijah; Abijah begot Asa; Asa begot Jehoshaphat . . .

The name of the person who interests us comes at the end of the list. He was filtered through each of those Israelites with profiles like goats and bitumen-coloured beards, who only on rare occasions were kindly or shone like angels. Men in whom dwelt the pride of the Jews; men without languor or melancholy, only gloom and expectation.

King David, Solomon, Jehoshaphat . . . High, towering names; names for hymns or famous stories woven on tapestries or painted on ceilings. But what about the obscure ones? *Jehoshaphat begot Joram; Joram, Azariah; Azariah, Jotham; Jotham, Ahaz* . . . Who was Azariah? Was he some incestuous fellow? Who was Jotham? A murderer? I don't know and I don't want to go into it; he too bore on his back a part of the man who interests us.

Manasseh begot Amon; Amon begot Josiah; Josiah begot Jeconiah and his brothers at the time of the deportation to Babylon.

Each time one of these men spurted out his seed, the one who interests us made a step towards us; among a thousand arabesques of generations he moved forward in the network of mysterious and preordained crossbreedings; he came on as inexorably as spring.

And after the deportation to Babylon . . . Achim begot Eliud, Eliud begot Eleazar, Eleazar begot Matthan . . .

The expectation, the great breathless expectation which oppressed the soul of Jewry was measured out in this list of names, each enumerated one by one like a necklace fingered by a blind man to check the fragments of the jewel.

Matthan begot Jacob; Jacob begot Joseph, the husband of Mary.

Come on, Matthew. And who did Joseph beget? But here the necklace breaks off. Joseph was a virgin.

So he didn't have children?

A DOWN-AT-HEEL GENTLEMAN

The person who interests us is Joseph. Joseph was chaste, noble, and a carpenter.

Chaste. At the estuary of such a torrent of fertility and of so many conceptions came a man who didn't beget, who didn't conceive; a dried-up man whose skin resembled his reserve and whose hands had touched only bread, wood, leather, cloth for clothes and the cinders in the hearth.

Noble. But he wasn't like any of his ancestors. Solomon's wisdom and David's boldness had flowed down to him through the veins of the ages but he had dissolved them into an innocent forgetfulness; and so he purged the sullen southern lust of Israel (which struck Solomon like lightning and blinded David too) in a virginity which was rather like a childhood that never waned. He was to grow old in that childhood as in a transparent wrapping. Without cracking in the gales of manhood, he came royally to the rewards of age free from all passion, always with the rather pallid colouring we associate with men confined to workshops.

For Joseph was a carpenter, *faber lignarius*. And that explains a lot. Wood is a strange, noble material, no longer earth and not yet flesh; just as milk isn't blood, yet is more than water. Wood is sensitive and chaste and Joseph exercised his innocent sensuality by passing his open palms along planks smoothed by his carpenter's plane, by caressing the edges bevelled by his lathe, and breathing in his nostrils the fragrance of sawdust – that odour of hard work which, whenever anyone comes to the door, makes a man raise his sweaty brow knowing that his visitor is a friend. Wood is goodness.

The person who interests us is Joseph the carpenter, the guardian chosen in the depths of the heavens. He could act as guardian precisely because he was a dreamer, he could keep watch because he was absorbed, he could be wary because he was guileless, he could guide because he was inexperienced.

DAYS AND NIGHTS

Something very difficult happened in the life of this most transparent of men.

Mary . . . was betrothed to Joseph and before they came together she found she was with child . . .

All Judea, with its habit of stoning adulteresses, roared around Joseph and his fate, and the nerves and thoughts of this upright man who hammered nails were in turmoil. Scandal, mocking cruel scandal, in a land that couldn't feel compassion, couldn't smile, but could only condemn.

Days of torment. Joseph's pain did not lie in feeling he was a laughing-stock in a puritan city, nor in the resentment of a man cuckolded, nor in the heartbreak at the loss of his woman. His was a nobler pain; that of discovering that the creature he believed to be the best in the world was fallible; shame when he went out and when he stayed at home; the anguish of a man who wants to forgive what it's illegal to forgive, and who hesitates between the horror of harming the woman and the weapon of repudiation placed in his hands by imperious society to defend his honour.

He was alone with his wood in the shadow of the workshop. Everything seemed the same, with the plane sliding and the saw humming as the drama swelled in his heart. And there, surrounded by his wood, Joseph found a compromise.

But Joseph her husband, who was a man of principle and didn't want to expose her, decided to have the marriage contract quietly set aside.

DREAMS

Joseph, like other chaste souls, was a dreamer. The dreams of such transparent creatures are like dew which does good during the night and which only the glare of the midday sun altogether dispels.

The prelude to Matthew's Gospel is crisscrossed with such dreams (we still come across the philanthropic angel of the Old Testament, the angel who's always on his toes). They were white, tender dreams into which the swords of the wicked seemed to sink as into feathers . . . *an angel of the Lord appeared to Joseph and said, 'Get up, take the child and his mother and fly to Egypt and stay there until I let you know; for Herod's looking for the child to kill him';* and also frankly mocking dreams: *As they were warned in a dream not to revisit Herod, they returned to their country by another way* (and the mages or astrologers decamped on the swaying backs of their camels, having neatly duped the tetrarch).

Joseph was always dreaming. As soon as he was asleep his breathing became regular like footsteps into mysterious lands where the worker is expected every night to watch and listen. Whereas on these nights he had a weight on his heart, and his sleep was restless with tears and anger.

And then through the goodwill of a nocturnal friend his anxiety was changed into joy, the nightmare dissolved into

22

that happiness we can only experience when a death sentence is repealed, or when lost wealth is restored intact.

'Joseph, son of David, don't be afraid of taking your wife Mary with you; because the child she has conceived is the work of the Holy Ghost.'

So you're pure; I can take you into my house.

GOOD-BYE, JOSEPH

But now we say good-bye, Joseph, innocent fiancé from Galilee; good-bye to your dream of love. After that joyful news from heaven you found the angel's next words obscure: *'She'll give birth to a son . . . he'll save people from their sins.'*

From now on your life was to be one of long silence, and of slow understanding of that puzzling phrase. Understanding the meaning of your difficult destiny: the girl on whom your eyes had fallen as a young working-man; the girl for whom you sacrificed a marriage which you hoped would be simple and uneventful; the girl who entered your house . . . Understanding your wife, understanding your son, understanding yourself, Joseph, yourself – predestined to be our first saint.

From now on we'll hear no more about you. A few pages, and there's no further mention of your name. The gospel swallows you up. We just glimpse your hands on the carpenter's plane, just hear the muffled grinding of your saw, for who knows how many years. And then we find you again on the altars of churches, in bedside pictures, in pious statues, rugged and grey as though you'd always been old. We prefer to forget that when you were with Mary you were a strong and handsome young man; a young man in love.

YOU'LL CALL HIM JESUS

So Mary no longer belonged to Joseph. The great Rival whom the angel mentioned in the dream – the Rival whose presence was only dimly felt by the carpenter because of the satisfaction he'd been given by the words 'don't be afraid of taking her

23

with you' – had asked for her hand and despatched the same messenger to her.

That unknown messenger had appeared to her at the moment when an early-riser tiptoes through a sleeping house and stands by the window in secret kinship with the morning air and the birds. She was doing those little jobs that a woman who is always at home does to fill in the dead hours, occupying now her soul, now her hands.

It was the most propitious hour for receiving a message. And there stood Gabriel before her. He had chosen the most indefinite moment of that solitude, like someone who waylays his victim in the quietest corner of a wood.

'*I hail you, full of grace.*'

We begin the prayer with 'Hail Mary'. But the angel didn't mention her name. When two people are alone together, to call a virgin by her name is to touch her; the syllables of 'Mary' would have cracked the purity of that crystalline morning.

The angelic friend went on with courteous reassurances. He wanted the mystical rape to do as little harm as possible: '. . . *the Lord is with you, you are blessed among women, don't be afraid because you've found grace before God*' – but her face was full of instincts and forebodings; it was moved by more than the presence of the unknown stranger; so it was more generous that he should *speak*, should go straight to the kernel of the fateful news: '*Behold you'll conceive and give birth to a son and you'll call him Jesus.*'

Jesus. Now the angel's job was over. Jesus came into the world in that moment, with the two syllables which beat in the air in the room. His mission was now over, there was no getting away from that name. 'You'll call him Jesus.' He'd thrown that son-word into her lap, and with the name a whole story that the mother could read in her clairvoyant heart – from her first caress of the infant under the stable roof, to the cross, to the triumphant morning of the resurrection, to the cries of the holy and the hopeless who would appeal to her until the end of time.

But the virgin wasn't defeated; her answer wasn't that of

a mother but of an amazon: *'But how can this happen, considering I haven't been with a man?'* Where did this homely girl find the courage to talk of her own virginity and refer to what goes on between the sexes? In fact what she said was less a question than a secret torn open. 'I haven't been with a man' meant 'let me never go with one, take this cup away from me. The man I'm betrothed to has grasped this through love, will you please understand it too.'

THE PACT

So there were strange things under that roof, strange loves in that daughter of Joachim and Anna, who was little more than a child who got up at dawn. Angel, you arrived late. Someone had already visited her for a moment more secret still, and they had made a pact of virginity together. Virginity is the madness that no one then knew, the heresy no one then living could conceive of: having a body and not giving it to anyone, a vineyard of flesh closed to caresses. The vestal virgins fled and hid in the hills when they were chosen for their barbarous renunciation. For virginity is like blindness; a virgin's whole body hurts, down to the ends of her hair, as if virginity were an unendurable wound. Mad Mary was the first to choose this fruit so hateful to human beings. On that day God himself was amazed at her; and that day, possibly years before the angel appeared, the divine pregnancy began and the infant had a nest on the earth.

AN EYELESS MONSTER

'The Holy Ghost will come down on you and the power of the Most High will cover you with its shadow, and so the Holy One you'll give birth to will be called the Son of God.'

So it wasn't a man who was to cover her, but a shadow: a

very high shadow from the towers of heaven would tunnel into her belly, falling from dizzy heights, higher than eagles, higher than angels.

O Mary, what a terrible monster was to lie with you! No woman would have agreed to copulate with the sea and its tempests, with the zodiac of unknown stars, with the ether full of thunder and the sand encrusted with shells. A woman dreams of a mate who'll caress her so as to chase away her fear of the universe, who'll give her a house where she can hide and sleep. But you . . . you accepted that spouse without limits and without eyes to see you, hidden in all things and yet so cruelly far away, and you gave your answer: yes.

'Behold the handmaid of the Lord; be it done to me according to your word.'

ABOUT GOOD PEOPLE AND OTHERS

And so you became the mother of our fears and our resignations, the mother of sailors threatened with shipwreck, of travellers lost in mountains, of wounded soldiers, of sons without a mother, of mothers without their sons, of men who no longer have a home or bread or God.

I've known plenty of people who don't pray to your son but are in love with you, and, secretly, make grotesque and desperate vows to you. I've seen medals with your image round the necks of prostitutes and criminals, or tattooed – your hands joined in prayer – on the skin of the wretched and the blasphemous. I have heard your name millions of times – Mary the Virgin, Holy Madonna! – on the lips of all the men and women I know: said in anger or irritation or surprise, said on receiving good news or bad, said by someone who's nearly taken a tumble, said at a death, said for no reason at all. Always your name.

I know your shrines on plains and up mountains, so full of silver hearts, crutches and gory bandages that one can't see a square inch of the wall. I know the waters you've caused to pour into the wounds of the unfortunate just because a shepherd's child knelt down and prayed to you in a lonely ravine.

What's the meaning of your presence among us, in our tears and in the songs we sing you, ever since that early morning? What do we expect from our mutual embrace deriving from our hope and our superstition? Is it that when you're near, the division into categories of good and bad people is over, and we all accept one another in our common childhood, in the peaceful name of sons and daughters? Is it that the son you gave us, when you bowed before the angel's gentle and fearful command, is a mystery that in turn fascinates and repels us? But you, earthy little sister, who underwent your fate as we undergo ours, who cooked and sewed for a son who was doomed to die on you – you're like us; you're life's highest victim, that's all, and the most resigned one. You, Mary, lead the way in our misfortunes; and when we think we're praying to you it isn't prayer: it's going into your room at Nazareth and telling you we've hurt ourselves by being born and by living (as we did with our other mother), confident that you can do something for us, or at least answer.

THE FIRST PROCESSION

This was the one that Our Lady carried out alone, across Galilee, as far as the little green valleys of 'Ain Karim.

In those days Mary set out and went straight to a town in the mountains of Judea.

She joined up with the caravans, passed through the crowds in the city, and no one recognized her. She wasn't a statue made of wood or marble like the ones multitudes of people have knelt before for centuries. In Italy today, when a statue of her passes by, the traffic stops, the police push back the crowds, and people at their windows or on the doorsteps of their shops look perhaps gay, perhaps embarrassed, put out their cigarettes, cut short a laugh. Crowds follow her up into the hills holding canopies or torches, they trample poppies and narcissi underfoot and sing their passionate hymns.

But on that occasion Our Lady was alive, she was there, the secret of her body concealed beneath the veil that no painter has ever lifted for us. No one noticed her, she was just another woman in the crowd. Tradesmen hawked their wares; the merry went on laughing, the quarrelsome went on shouting. In the rough crowd of Jerusalem many brushed past that belly that wasn't yet visibly swollen – as they brushed past thousands of other things that day: a whore's tunic, a crate of dates, a camel's rump. They passed by her in the heedless and greedy to-ing and fro-ing of their daily affairs, and each of them, even the merriest, had somewhere within him the eternal thought: supposing something happened . . . supposing someone were going to arrive . . .

But when she reached her destination, up in Elizabeth's house, her incognito was broken; someone recognized her, the procession became real, like ours now, when in the streets everyone says, 'It's the Madonna'.

And it happened that as soon as Elizabeth heard Mary's greeting, the child leapt in her womb and Elizabeth was filled with the Holy Ghost and raised her voice and cried, 'You are blessed among women and blessed is the fruit of your womb'.

THE KICK OF JOY

Who was this first human being to meet Jesus and recognize him? A man of thorny destiny, a belated prophet, a character who seems out of place and without an explanation.

Ageing Elizabeth – you didn't realize that you'd conceived miraculously in the twilight of your life so as to give birth to that lean, grave son who would dress in goatskins and live on grass and insects in the desert, and, as had been foretold, would drink no wine nor any intoxicating liquor. By now it was getting a bit late to take up the career of a prophet; the time was at hand for apostles. And it was absurd to admonish adulterous kings with the ancient law of 'thou shalt not' when soon the new law would melt in a glance hearts more corrupt than your Herod's. O John the Baptist, the paths of the Lord

28

which you wanted to straighten were never to be finished, and your head would fall into the dark macabre dish as it had always lived and wouldn't be the cause of a single tear or a single regret.

But, John, your sombre, lonely life had one moment of joy. In the sunlight you never smiled, but once in the dark urn-like womb, where neither human threats nor the whistling wind could reach, you experienced a joy you couldn't contain; you encountered a friend enclosed in another womb.

'. . . *from the moment your greeting sounded in my ears, the baby kicked for joy in my womb.*'

This is the first time the word joy is mentioned in the Gospels and we owe it to you, doleful prophet. This is where the good news begins, with this invisible smile in the darkness of a womb.

CONVERSATION AT 'AIN KARIM

ELIZABETH: The angel appeared to Zacharias when he was burning incense in the sanctuary. He was standing in the cloud of smoke and they talked to one another through the wall of incense in the ancient odour of thuribles.

The angel announced that I'd have a baby called John, and he said a lot of nice things about John, but Zacharias was doubtful about what he said because he was thinking about his old age and my sterility. Then from inside the incense the angel said:

'*I am Gabriel, and I stand before God, and I've been sent to talk to you and tell you this happy news. And you'll be dumb and won't be able to talk until the day all these things happen because you didn't believe what I said.*' Zacharias has been dumb ever since, and things are silent in our house.

But now you've arrived, and you and I will be able to talk day and night.

MARY: We'll talk day and night. Give me your hands and leave them in mine. We have secrets fearful enough to make us tremble between the sheets, but we'll sleep in each other's arms. We'll tell all our thoughts to one another hundreds of times over while our sons in our wombs can't hear. Before they're born we can talk and weep and exult together for the last time. Afterwards it will stop. Oh let's get talking quickly – they are growing so quickly inside us and a superhuman job awaits them. Let's talk as much as we can while we're still alone and while our hands can weave wool and linen as usual, and while, when we go indoors or to the fountain, we can take them with us, for they won't belong to us any more once they can walk; they'll flee to the desert and walk on the waves of the sea.

ELIZABETH: I was sterile and have conceived. I used to be ashamed to eat any fruit because I hadn't produced any fruit; I felt I was stealing the shade from the plants, the air from the birds, and in springtime I shut myself up indoors because I felt everything around me was fertile. As soon as a mustard-seed fell from a sack a shrub sprang up, as soon as a bumble-bee alighted on a flower a flower-bed appeared, but as for me, I had a secret leprosy in my womb.

Now a man has sprung to life in my belly. I'll make eyes for him so that he can look at the violet sunsets over the domes of Jerusalem, a voice to frighten the antelopes in the desert, a backbone so that he can stand upright before the powerful; he'll have ten fingers on his hands strong enough to crack the toughest nutshells. And while I'm talking it's I who am weaving all these things round his grain of flesh, for I'm no longer sterile. *So you see what the Lord accomplished when he was kind enough to put an end to my humiliation among people.*

MARY: I'll go on staying in your house, I'll get to know the shadows the furniture makes as it follows the circle of the sun, the shutters where the gusts of wind are noisiest, the special creaking of the various doors, and the scent of every plant in the garden. I'll stay a long time until I've emptied my heart of fear and my soul becomes used to a joy that would kill the angels and drive rocks mad.

You must put your arms round me and have pity on my joy. Hold me tight while I sing once and for all what has been destined for me alone, little particle that I am.

AS IN A VALLEY

'*My soul glorifies the Lord and my spirit exults with joy in God, my saviour, because he has looked on the humility of his handmaid. And from now onwards all generations will call me blessed because the Almighty One, whose name is holy, has worked great things in me.*'

He has given me men. In my belly, as in a valley in the Bible, I feel you all moving, you countless billions of children of the earth, I know your names one by one, I count the hair on your heads as if you were sucking at my breast and as if nothing ran in your veins but my precious milk.

I'll be the most loved of women. The passionately devoted husband will prefer me to the girl sleeping beside him, the most devoted son will forget his mother for a thread of my gown, and the proudest kings will kneel down like slaves when they pronounce my name.

Children will prefer me to their games, soldiers to their wars, sailors to the sea, lovers to their mistresses' lips, the dying to life. I'll be the Virgin. The tiniest of your sorrows will pass within me like the breath of the faintest wind in a sail, and I shall gather it into the hollow of my hands and breathe my merciful breath on it. For everyone I'll be pity without judgment or calculation, indulgence without rancour or conditions, the one who'll want to see you happy at every moment solely because you call me mother.

I look at my hands in which he has placed a treasure of countless graces and I'd like to pour them all out over the most ungrateful among you for a single ejaculatory prayer. I look at my feet, and from the tower to which his mighty arm has raised me, I see below your burning altars in their thousands upon thousands, like the lights on ships in distress. And my soul glorifies the Lord who chose me to answer you and say that you are safe.

HOW MANY WERE THERE?

And it happened that in those days Caesar Augustus sent out a ukase for a census of all the empire.

Caesar wanted to know how many there were. So he made preparations for counting them, sent out his ukase, and mobilized with dire penalties huge crowds on the roads of an empire that was frightening in its immensity. There they were in Thrace, in Illyria, in Mesopotamia; in Greece, in Africa, in Spain; in the land of the Parthians, the Britons and the Scythians – a swarm of human herds toiling along in their multi-coloured footgear. They were off to be counted. The emperor wanted to know how many there were, how many people adored him. And he thought he had counted them all.

But there was one subject who wasn't counted, his card was missing in the thousands of urns. Augustus's smooth handsome face showed no concern; in such an endless multitude, one more, one less . . .

Soon he noticed that the sum didn't add up, that the census had made a mistake.

'How on earth,' Caesar asked, 'how on earth?'

And yet the praetors, functionaries and scrutineers had been hard-working and meticulous. 'You can take it, your Divinity, that the census was perfect.'

'Odd,' said Caesar, 'for the numbers don't add up. Someone wasn't counted.'

THE SECOND PROCESSION

And they all went to give in their names, each in his own town.

The second procession was from Nazareth to Bethlehem. This time people noticed Mary – she was so obviously pregnant, and (what with the weight in her body, step after step, for miles and miles) so obviously exhausted!

But those were uncomfortable, tiring days for everyone; the census had mobilized every family in the whole of Galilee down to the children and the sick; and all of them, torn away from the daily round, deprived of the tiny comforts of home life, had their burden of heat, thirst, hunger and bad-temper – they had lost all forbearance and all concern for others. Quarrels broke out at crossroads, some became thieves ready to grab the water-bottles of others, and even the humblest and most honest – who at home accorded a high place to kindness and amiability – now on the lizard-infested roads curled up inside themselves and calculated the tiny advantages they could obtain without yielding an inch on their side. They said, 'Tomorrow we'll be kind again; on the way back.'

It was thus that Mary went on her second procession, with eyes avoiding her for fear of having to offer help. Other pregnant women had been observable during these days. It was up to their husbands . . .

And by evening, when weariness stuck needles into their limbs, the men turned into wolves to get a bed (for in the East nights are damp and cold); teeth and claws had to be bared if some lair was to be found. But Joseph and Mary lacked claws. They were dreamy and didn't notice that the hunt for places to doss down had long started – with money, cunning and tears.

So those who were behindhand came to blows; they fought with fists and oaths over the last bit of straw, the last corner under a portico. Between the turquoise sky and the dusty white road the spider of night wove his web more and more thickly. Dusk came on as with every night, placidly; the first bat flitted over the gardens, then came the mosquitoes, then the owl stretched on his branch, and then people became voices and sex within the lit-up houses. This night was just like any other. There was no knowing it was *the* night.

Suddenly they found they were alone. Their travelling companions had disappeared to the last man and woman, without a word of farewell.

BETTER THAT WAY

. . . because there was no room for them in the inn.

They asked for just a little space. They didn't ask rich people enclosed in their rooms with the fragrance of braziers; they asked the poorest who were crowded into the courtyard, those who could recognize their wilting eyes, those who knew the torture of passing a night on the freezing ground without a spark of fire.

Possibly it would have been enough to push aside a donkey, or that huddle of dice-players could have squeezed up, and with coats and haversacks a hard bed could have been improvised for the woman swollen with child, and the man could remain standing. But limbs are so comfortable when torpor sets in – everyone was savouring the pleasure of weariness shifting from their legs like a gentle bloodletting. It was each for himself and God for all.

They didn't know how near to them that 'God for all' was passing, and yet in a few hours he would come into the world for them too: for those people stretched out in the inn, who had opened one eye to look at his mother, but hadn't even bothered to get up to shut the door behind her.

Mary sighed. She still had to move her feet; that stable was still a long way off. But secretly it was a sigh of relief; because the baby wouldn't be born here, surrounded by the sweat and sham snoring of the cheats and ruffians, the boorish selfishness of the first arrivals.

THE END OF DREAMS

There were shepherds spending the night out of doors and guarding their sheep.

But there were others stretched out on the ground . . . and

these had leapt to their feet, stamped out the remains of their bivouac, and started to run.

The angel had come to Mary in the hour preceding dawn, when the house was as limpid as an aquarium, the blood swift and pure in the veins; but to the shepherds the angel came in the hour of fire, when men have stared into its embers to the point of intoxication and are possessed by a heavy dullness. The angel fell like a falcon on the contentment of these dreaming men, their eyes half-closed, their skin warmed by the glow, and smashed like a rock through the web of their meditations which long delay had made ever more complicated and abstruse.

It's fine being shepherds, the fire is fine, so are the sheep ruminating under the stars, the milk that swells their udders and the wool that grows on their backs. And then there are those moonlight nights round the fire when memory swells and reaches as far as the shores of childhood and even farther, back to ancestral legends . . . It was a temptation, the reveries of these men; one more pinnacle, one more volute or frieze, and it would have been a sin.

Up you get, shepherds. Tonight someone has been born for you, too, to break up your bivouacs and chase you from the delicious kingdom of expectation.

And the angel said to them: *'Don't be afraid, for I'm announcing to you a great joy which is intended for everyone; today in David's city a saviour is born and he's the Christ . . .'*

Human sheep, come to pasture; a herd that bites and won't leave its shepherd in peace. Come and see him.

SPACE AND TIME

Let's go and see him. Let's go back through the seemingly immense distance, let's climb down the tower of nearly two thousand Christmases between us and him. There are still warm embers of last Christmas beneath the ashes of the months and we still recall the table-cloth gaily laid out, the places occupied by the others at dinner and all the various dishes, the

35

gay presents bought in a hurry during Advent when the whole city seems like a mad liner that may haul up its anchor at any moment. On these occasions people turn into ants trying to drag into their anthill as much stuff as they can, and on Christmas eve they wall themselves up in their nests and block every cranny so that happiness won't escape.

Let's go down, down, back to the earliest Christmases of our childhood which are iridescent in our memories like a gentle obsession, when [in Italy] men with reed-pipes and bagpipes came down from the mountains to bewitch our young hearts. In those days our hearts were charged with a secret madness which lasted until the Christmas tree was dismantled, and only then the gold-dust fell from our eyes.

But Bethlehem is still a long way away: a forest of centuries stands between our births and his. Lucky shepherds, you only needed to cross a hillside, perhaps a torrent-bed, a quarter-of-an-hour's walk or so. Whereas we need to leap over history, a fortified wall of enormous thickness which your birth-cry can't penetrate, nor the chorus of spirits, to us who are born so late. All we have left – we who are excluded – are nostalgic paintings by Correggio and Fra Bartolommeo. Or else we have to be rebellious poets and take our head between our hands and break down the pitiless bastion by blows of the skull.

I'm going to see him. The journey lasts nearly two thousand years; I'm joining up as a volunteer in that dead story, in those ashes of the ages, solely so as to meet him. I take on the flesh of as many bodies as necessary to have the body of one of those shepherds, his ears hot from the fire, the wind from Galilee in his hair, the creaking of the steppe beneath his feet, the breadth of his back in the narrow space of the stable, that tumultuous *now* within the walls of his heart inundated by mystery.

TWELVE WORDS

. . . *they found Mary and Joseph and the baby lying in the manger.*

That's all. The twelve-worded Christmas crib comes from Luke the evangelist who never saw it himself, any more than his master Paul of Tarsus saw it: only those nocturnal shepherds pulverized into nothingness. Three names and a piece of farm equipment. Let us, too, make the crib small and real. We read and reread those twelve words – as we pore over a diamond until we tarnish it with our breath. There lies our whole Christmas. The words were written by a doctor from Antioch whose pen never trembled with the temptation to say more.

NAKED AND MAD

But we'll say more. We'll dance with our mad words round the baby. We'll go and find him and those nearest will buzz around him like bees, and those farthest away will press their mouths to the ground and chew the grass. We'll be a crowd of condemned men cut down from the scaffold at the very last moment. Each of us will say his twenty or thirty words giving a précis of his life – the names of living people and dead, horrible fears and stubborn hopes – each will give birth to himself.

It'll be a huge business, stripping ourselves naked and looking at ourselves on that hillside. The murderer and the saint, the old man and the boy, the rich and the poor, he who thought himself wretched and he who said he was happy, all will measure out with dismay the short step separating them: the fear of death, the hunger for salvation that made them equal.

The salvation born that night among our rocks makes us laugh and tremble. We feel we have a well-caulked ship beneath our feet and the sea can't swallow us up. We feel the salt of incorruptibility beneath our skin. We exchange unshaven embraces.

All's afire tonight in this straw hut. And the unendurable blaze makes us seek refuge and defence in childlike happiness.

Only one person can hold out in the happy pyre. He looks at us and repeats an ancient promise fulfilled by himself: '*It's my joy to be with the sons of men.*'

THE SAINTS OF GOLD

Once Jesus had been born, mages or astrologers from the East appeared in Jerusalem saying, 'Where is the child born to be king of the Jews? For we saw his star in the East and have come to adore him.'

Why had he made them come from such a distance? He had made their camels bellow as they crouched in their stalls in Transjordania and in the stables of Persia and Mesopotamia; he had made them struggle to their feet at the hoarse cry of the camel-drivers at night; he had pricked their flanks with the spur of that star galloping towards the West.

Why did he want them? Weren't the Judean shepherds enough, poor and ignorant like their sheep, with whom his mother could exchange homely words without shyly hiding her breast?

These men were so rich that they wouldn't have stooped to pick up a pearl, so wise that no book would have made them raise an eyebrow. They spoke a foreign tongue that his mother couldn't understand when they entered the kitchen at Bethlehem – where she had found refuge with her tiny son – and the stamping feet of their retinue in the courtyard frightened her, and their mantles of woven silk trailing over the rough floor put her to shame.

Why had he given them the inconvenience of travelling from their luxurious closets hung with tapestries impregnated with resin, and why stirred hearts that had hitherto beaten evenly beneath robes flawlessly embroidered?

Why had he shaken them out of their lethargy of wisdom, now that their calculations had counted the stars in the heavens and the grains of sand in the desert?

So it isn't even true that he hated the rich, though he was to say that it's harder for the rich to win him than for a camel to pass through the eye of a needle . . .

And it isn't true either that learned men bored him, though he was to say that the kingdom of heaven was for the simple . . .

What repels him is the rich man who can't get up at night, open his coffers and bring gifts to an unknown baby; and the doctrine of those who think it's stupid to follow the caprices of a star, of those who have wiped the word 'adore' from their vocabulary.

Whereas the astrologers, by a very rare miracle wrought by his angels, had become holy despite their wealth and learning.

Their cheeks perfumed with myrrh and spikenard were fit to press his innocent cheeks, and their hands were fit to caress him without their having to remove a single ring.

THE DEAL

And the star they saw in the East went before them until it stood over the place where the baby was. Now when they saw the star they became very joyful. And when they reached the house and saw the baby with Mary his mother, they fell down in adoration; and they opened their coffers and gave him gifts of gold, incense and myrrh.

Two deals can be made if we want to regain our youth: Faust's deal and the infant Jesus' deal. Like Goethe's old doctor, these elderly astrologers – as their life was drawing to a close – struck a deal: they bartered seventy years of philosophical habits for the naïvety of this hare-brained journey, the contents of their coffers for this squandering in the depths of the unknown, the dignity of their halls where everyone paid them homage for the absurdity of a trip on the backs of dromedaries and the embarrassment of having to ask sarcastic passers-by and a conceited monarch: 'Where is the child born to be king?'

But in the kitchen with Mary and Joseph, among the cloths hung out to dry, you gave them a handsome reward. In exchange for their royal appurtenances you gave their childhood back to Gaspar, Melchior and Balthasar – their sweet childhood which had long been hidden beneath the abstruse calculations of Zarathustra and the icy compasses of the Chaldeans; the very stainless and gentle childhood that let you play with their

39

solemn beards, their gold bracelets and their grains of incense as though they were sycamore leaves or pebbles in a brook. Then the three new children put their feet once more in the stirrups and mounted the beasts on which they'd come. Their long caravan, winding its way back, tied West and East together by the thread of youth.

THOSE AT THE APPOINTMENT

But the baby had been embraced by other hands before the arrival of the astrologers. The third procession happened forty days after his birth and was from Bethlehem to Jerusalem where Mary had to go for the rite of purification. Joseph carried on his wrist the two turtle-doves of the offering and in his palm the five pieces of silver for the ransom of a first-born child.

Solomon's temple seemed to have been built by God – that massive structure, pink in the morning light, with huge stones that only his hand could have placed for the comings and goings of such swarms of people. It seemed crowded out – stall-keepers and scribes had stuffed it so full of merchandise and chatter – but really it was almost empty; in fact only two people really lived in it, Simeon the sacristan and Anna the devout old woman, and for them this wasn't an ordinary day. Like Elizabeth and the unborn John, like the shepherds and the astrologers, they too kept the appointment; the few intimates whom the Lord – with an angel's message or a star or the Holy Ghost – had invited secretly to the first supper of salvation: birthday creatures approved from on high.

Anna was a widow countless years old. She had made her nest in the temple like an old swallow that doesn't want ever to migrate again, so that she had taken on the colour of the temple and was identical with its stones rusted over the centuries. Yet within that faded soul there burned a rare flame, the flame of prophecy: *she spoke of him to everyone who was waiting for the liberation of Jerusalem.*

That day the infant rewarded her. He threw a gem into the

chaff of her days, he descended into her weary old arms with
the restless weight of a creature that has only just felt the
beating air. And Anna, her eyes closed, smelt him. Her nostrils
recognized in those swaddling clothes the strange dark odour
of God.

JOY AND SORROW

Simeon wasn't a priest. He was an ordinary man who had been
conscientious all his life and only wanted to die. His affairs
had been in order for countless years and he had said good-bye
to his friends. His larder never contained an extra fruit for the
morrow. In his breast death was ripe like a pear that bends the
bough with its weight.

He was waiting for his day to come, that good day when
his eyes would close, when he'd no longer need to knot his
turban and light a fire that no longer kept him warm, but only
stretch himself out, rub off the colours of here-below and
float in light. But he still had to wait. He had an appointment
with someone who was late but wouldn't fail to turn up. He
had prepared the short speech he would make:

'*Now, Master, let your servant depart – according to your word – in
peace! Because my eyes have seen your salvation, that you have prepared
before all the peoples.*'

His joy as he held him in his arms beneath the atrium of the
temple was unlike Anna's. For him it was like pardon granted
to a prisoner, a door opening. Let him go, Lord. Quick; let
him die before he's said the other words, because these will
change this lovely day of sun and turtle-doves into a gloomy
vigil for your mother; you'll never see her smile again after
that.

'*This child is destined to bring about the fall of many and the rise
of many in Israel and to be a sign of contradiction; and so the thoughts
of many hearts will be made public, and your soul too will be pierced
by a sword.*'

CHORUS OF THE INNOCENTS

Meanwhile when Herod saw he'd been deceived by the wise men, he got into a furious rage and gave orders to murder all the male children under two in Bethlehem and its area, according to the time that he'd carefully found out from the wise men.

We were the babies of Bethlehem. You babies of all the earth and all the ages, you should have envied us because for us the baby Jesus really came; our parents had no need to prepare a cradle for us, all that was needed was arms to lift us up to the window – with the addition of a slit in our tiny throats. But our parents wept so much.

To us the baby didn't bring a toy horse with a flaxen mane, or a drum with green and red tassels, or vanilla-flavoured cakes. He brought us a macabre game which can only be played for a moment and afterwards no other game is possible. We'd never heard its name before: it was called death.

We are the babies of Bethlehem: we had tiny hands like his which were beginning to feel things, and little voices like his that grated like chips of glass on the usual noises of the house, and when we first began to walk our mothers, like his, had no more peace for fear we'd fall into the water or the fire.

Our mothers wept long hours over a nasty cut on our fingers, and our fathers shouted at them quite crossly. Now we have enormous cuts in our throats made by the soldiers' swords.

Those lovely, shiny swords, far better than our little tin ones, and those lovely leather belts with chains and buckles such as we'd never seen and which it would have been marvellous to play with.

And we thought it was a game when they took us from our cradles in their hairy arms, except that we heard our mothers howling more than on the day we were born.

So we began crying too, but only because our mothers did, because we were used to imitating them spontaneously in everything we saw them doing.

42

Then, though we were tiny, we suddenly realized that that was what it was: dying. Death for us was a wedge of truth in the soft unknowingness of childhood: it tore away our simplicity like a bandage from our eyes and we saw, in a flash, all the good years that Herod had robbed us of: the love of girls among the summer rushes of the Jordan, outings on Lake Tiberias, festivals in the temple, moonlight nights, children on our laps, and perhaps – for one or two of us – the company of Jesus of Nazareth. This made it rather painful.

But the moment we'd been killed all sorrow vanished. We suddenly knew that the baby was safe, travelling on an ass in his mother's arms to a country where they'd let him play; and that was our Christmas present. Our slit throats didn't hurt any more.

A BLANK PAGE

So that very night he got up, took the baby and his mother and sought refuge in Egypt where he stayed till Herod's death, so that what the Lord said through the prophet would be fulfilled: 'I've called my son out of Egypt.'

Of the sojourn in Egypt, however, we know nothing. Nothing. It's like a smooth lake between two shores, on whose waters the footprints of the holy family break off, disappear, as if to girdle this flight with jealous reserve through the centuries (perhaps Herod's ghost wasn't yet placated . . .).

So legend-weavers have embroidered this blank page with baroque webs – such as the wild beasts in the desert becoming tame and turning themselves into soft pillows for the fugitives to sleep on, the banana and date trees stooping to offer their fruit to the baby's mouth, or Dismas, the good thief, who was to be crucified on his right hand, emerging from the sand-dunes and coming to their help. All we know, from historians' conjectures, is that the journey was a hard one, an expedition that had made Tiberius's well-equipped legions quail. But we know nothing of the child's time there; it's a gap in the gospel which we can fill in with all the freedom of our imagination.

After the anxiety and exhaustion of the flight, and the initial struggles of settling into a new home, might this not have been an oasis of peace, a transitory hard-won period of being safe, unharmed and unknown, in a circle of love made more magic by distance from the motherland? Was this the real short childhood of Jesus, with his games amid the age-old dust of the Pharaohs and the cats sacred to Osiris? Did he sleep sweetly, and was there that laughter in the eyes between mother and child when they first acknowledged one another on earth? Or perhaps in the evenings, when the pyramids threw a long shadow, alarm and gloom assailed the exiles and a nostalgia for Palestine tugged at their hearts, the land flowing with milk and honey on the other side of the desert, God's land where a large share had been allotted to them, with its olive groves and skull-shaped hills?

But news of Herod's death soon came. Archelaus now sat on the throne and Joseph decided to return home.

Let's put our finger on the atlas; Jesus was in this section of Africa. He passed by like a drop of mercury which leaves no mark, and we'll look for his traces in vain. O Egypt, curtain of enigmas, you absorbed into your millenary guts even a strip of this gospel which belongs to everyone.

THOSE THIRTY YEARS

He retired to the region of Galilee and went to live in the town called Nazareth.

Then Nazareth. Years like oars beating in the rowlocks of a boat. A poor man's house with daily hunger and daily bread, the night for sleep, the well for thirst; and for sadness, joy, affections, for all that – only silence. At a given hour all three sat round a table and munched, and gulps of wine went down their throats. After their last mouthful the two men got up and took up their tools again until nightfall. Then the shapes of three figures under the blankets, and their chests rising and falling in sleep.

I don't understand. I understand the incarnation, I understand the blind man being cured, the raising of Lazarus and all the miracles, I understand the soldier striking him, the crucifixion, death, Easter, and I understand him in the Host; but I don't understand those thirty years. I don't understand how it was him and not someone else who was in a band of breathless children chasing one another behind the walls of Nazareth, who hurried back home under the first drops of a downpour when doors and windows were slammed to. I don't understand his hair growing, the carpenter's plane slipping from his hands, the splinter that might prick him, or the passer-by who might bump into him or ask him the way. I don't understand how every day there emerged from his house, as from every other, a shovelful of refuse in which there gleamed white eggshells from which he had sucked, or possibly a soiled bandage on which his blood had splashed when he was using the saw.

It's easy to recognize him later; when he hadn't a stone to rest his head on, when he moved among the multitudes and every step he took made a prophecy come true, when he talked to his disciples and the Gospels seized on every word. But there in Nazareth, where he lay down every night in an ordinary bed, and went about the humble affairs of every day, and exchanged words that weren't about eternal life – what about that? Those thirty years . . .

I was thirty once. I lived at home as long as he did, I measured out the same number of hours and passed through the same stages as him – infancy, adolescence, puberty, young manhood. They were inexpressible years, with girls and landscapes, years that fermented like a bunch of grapes in the sun. What did he do during those thirty years?

The book reveals nothing (. . . *and Jesus grew*, Luke says). He wanted to impose even this test on us: that of believing that the Son of man was nothing but a young stay-at-home.

NAZARENE AND CHRIST

. . . so that what had been said through the prophets might be fulfilled, that he'd be called Nazarene.

Whereas I call him Nazarene and the gospel reassures me on the point. Even the thirty years spent in that obscure township were a fulfilment of the prophets, yet another description by which to recognize him.

That name, as sonorous as a cymbal, had been murmured in confidence by the Father centuries earlier into the ears of Elijah and Daniel; and before the world existed Nazareth was already there in the great white chorus of the angels so that he could call himself Nazarene.

Nazarene is the name of the patient and opaque incarnation, as Christ is the name of the heroic and dazzling incarnation. He wanted to be a man in times of triumph and torment, among the fanning palms, the sobs in the garden, the cries of the crucifixion. But for a longer period he wanted to live a commonplace life so as to be our companion in the mediocrity of ordinary working days; so that, in every solitary and insignificant moment, in every wretched and unwanted occupation, in the hidden places of our greyest hours, we would know that he had passed here too; he too loved the knife and the lantern, the chair and the fly, summer and winter.

So, when in my room in the evening I sink into my tiredness, which is lost in the hundred thousand tirednesses of the city, I don't call him Christ, I call him Nazarene: which means the God of any ordinary city, any ordinary house, any ordinary hour, and of these hands that have done one more day's work.

A DIVINE CAPRICE

At the end of the third day they found him in the temple sitting in
the midst of the doctors, busy listening to them and questioning them,
and all who heard him were full of amazement at his intelligence and
his answers.

But one day there was a surprise, a day that was different.
Their house was empty because they had gone to Jerusalem
for a feast-day. Joseph and Mary returned as it grew dark, but
separately – he with the men's caravan, she with the women's.
Each thought mistakenly that the child was with the other.
They met on the doorstep. 'Where's Jesus?'

They were pale, each silently blaming themselves. And they
set out for the city again.

'I'm a bad guardian', Joseph was thinking.

'Perhaps his hour has come already,' Mary was thinking,
'perhaps it's all begun.'

A three days' hunt. Once again the two of them were tramp-
ing along the roads.

The child was in the temple. He was there with his short
tunic and his small face in an intaglio of light, together with
all the others hidden behind big beards and huge sleeves. The
doctors of Israel were the opposite of the astrologers. Their
doctrine had calcified on their backs like an enormous tortoise-
shell, and their hearts were as hardened as coral. They were the
rich who wouldn't get up at night and wouldn't follow a
comet. They mentioned Moses, Elijah and Jeremiah as though
they were quoting articles from the penal code. For their
God was a book, and man was a thing they'd never given a
thought to. Jesus knew that they were the furthest from salvation, that perhaps for the majority of them he would be nailed
up in vain. One or two of them would probably take part in
the plot twenty years later. Yet he'd wanted to visit them before
anyone else. He'd caused pain to his mother for the sake of those
superstitious blockheads who on the sabbath wouldn't brush

47

a fly away from their noses and would let their oxen drown in a well.

The gospel mentions only one convert among these doctors – the best of them, Nicodemus, who was to visit the Master by night for fear of being seen, was to listen to him wide-eyed, stammer the most comic words in the gospel, and go away rubbing his ears. But for all present the child had escaped from home, passed three days with them away from the warmth of Nazareth and in the planetary cold of their erudite words. We needn't be surprised at his learning: he spoke of books he himself had dictated to the prophets. What surprises us is the man-hunting, the pursuit in advance of the least deserving – giving himself up to be devoured like bread even by the most disagreeable mouths. Still today love is a source of wonderment to us.

WHY HAVE YOU DONE THIS TO US?

When they saw this they were amazed and his mother said to him: 'My son, why have you done this to us? For, you see, your father and I have been looking for you in anguish.' And he answered: 'Why were you looking for me? Didn't you know that I had to go about my Father's business?' But they didn't understand . . .

And we can't understand either. We call ourselves your chosen and loved ones, and we'd like you to grow up in our house and say, 'I'm going out, I'll be back at such-and-such a time'. We'd like to keep you in a cage like a chaffinch with seed and water-dishes, wall you up in a corner; and that's why we manufacture plaster sacred-hearts and glass cases and feed you with candles. We're in love with you only because you look so handsome with your soft eyes under hair divided by a thin parting and a fair beard; because your birth was so full of poetry and your death so moving: but we haven't understood a thing about you as Christ. It's one of our agelong sins to want you to dine with us as you did with Simon the Leper, so we can satisfy our curiosity by looking at you; to send for you as though you were a famous surgeon; to put our dead into your arms as into an embalmer's, so that you'll see to it that we find them intact and smiling in that vague place we call paradise. But you forgive us and sympathize with us and with the trumpery we call faith; with the margin left over from our selfishness that we call love. We're poor snails living in a shell: we still make a distinction between friends and enemies, between the living and the dead; we're afraid of pain as our hand is afraid of a reptile; and all this goes to show that we've learnt nothing from you.

The only prayer that would come to our lips, as it did to your mother's, if we found you at last, would be one of unconscious grievance: 'Why have you done this to us?'

The first part of the gospel closes on this theme of flight, on the empty house, and in an outburst of hard pitiless words. Once it was like that for each of us, too; when childhood was stripped of its happy days, its peaceful nights. In a flash you were no longer in the house; Nazareth was swept away. You had to be hunted down in the most repulsive places, in the hovels of down-and-outs, in distant regions among savages, in the faces of the dead: in that city of the oppressed called Jerusalem.

And you never appear to us when our unbelieving fingers want to feel the wounds you showed to Thomas; you no longer halt our funeral processions to say to us, as you did to the widow of Nain: 'He's alive, stop crying.' You went away, Lord. Nazareth was our childhood, too, and now your business is our business. Your reasons aren't ours, but you go on saving us in a hard and incomprehensible way, because we know that one day we'll admit you're right and everything will be restored to us.

Only leave us your name, Jesus Christ, so that we can repeat it when all other words have become extinguished: your name like a pearl in the valves of our mouth; and arms to embrace the people you've given us as brothers, in a tangle like a forest of ivy. Then put out the sun and the other stars and do with us what you like.

STRAIGHTAWAY

. . . he left the Jordan and straightaway the Spirit drove him into the desert so he might be tempted by the Devil.

So his life was beginning. Jesus had only just been baptized by John in the waters of the river, as we were baptized with the additional festivity of bright-coloured cakes, emotional aunts and toast-drinking. What was the meaning of that ceremony? The priest said some words that some of the people present couldn't understand, but now and again a more comprehensible expression would crop up – *Devil* – so among us there was a character with a hateful name, *maledicte diabule, immunde spiritus* . . . He wasn't a guest; on the contrary, he was excluded ('*Go out of him* . . .' '*hear your sentence of condemnation* . . .'). Baptizing a baby means beginning a duel with its enemy. And when the last words of the rite have faded on the air a childlike conviction radiates among the relatives and friends present – because such power is in that liturgy, and the baby has been washed in the blood of Christ, and because we find nothing more credible and reassuring than the words *te exorcizo* . . . *lineo te oleo salutis* – a conviction that Satan has been driven away, that *that* baby has escaped his clutches and so will live a good and happy life into old age. Look how peacefully he's sleeping in his lace . . . Let's drink a toast.

Whereas . . . *straightaway*. Even for Christ – as if to give the lie to the splendid words of the sacrament – the Evil One straightaway showed his hand. More than that, it was *the Spirit* that *drove* him into the desert *so he might be tempted by the Devil*. The Spirit provided Satan with ideal conditions for the enterprise. The desert. Where there's nothing: so that even the face and voice of my enemy – because it interrupts the horror of being alone – could seem the face and voice of a brother. Where fasting from all food and joy has put the weight of every sort of lust into my body. Where wild animals are at large (*in those days he was with wild beasts*). We're not really tempted by the veils of strippers; it's in the desert that we're tempted, with our own inner jackals and hyaenas, in that flat hell called loneliness.

So the Spirit doesn't take into account the optimism of our good parents who were smiling at our baptism. Straightaway he drives us out into the desert so as to be tempted.

Almost as soon as he'd emerged from tutelage in Nazareth, Christ's first gift to us was neither a miracle nor a parable. It was preceding us into the flames of Hate, sharing with us the law applying to every man born: temptation.

Christ tempted by Satan, Jesus tossed up and carried through the air in Satan's arms – this doesn't shock me. When I analyse the words and tactics of the three attempts to seduce Christ I get a rather weird conviction: that Satan had no clear idea of who he was dealing with. Like my creaturely self, Satan had only a confused and restricted idea of what the enigma of the incarnation was about. How *could* he have understood, however intelligent? Had he done so, where would he have found the courage to come near?

Satan, my brother in blindness, a dilettante in theology, an amateur in psychology, you know how to tempt *me*, a poor finite creature, with things like money and sex; but confronted with the Infinite Man there in that desert, you seem to have displayed a weariness and perplexity deriving from a job carried on over thousands upon thousands of years, and even in the impudence of your words I seem to detect some sort of strident inferiority complex.

Mammon knew Holy Scripture, and trembled with fear at the thought of a messiah burgeoning within human history. But was there any reason to believe in such an absurd promise? And even if there were, would the messiah be so mad as to leave his beatific state so as to insert himself within the distasteful exile of matter?

So he tried out provocative sallies against this suspect messiah. *'If you're the Son of God, turn those stones into bread.' 'If you're the Son of God, throw yourself over this precipice and the hands of angels will hold you up . . .'*

Christ as conjuror to get rid of hunger, Christ as acrobat on

51

the roofs of houses so as to amaze and conquer the crowd: that was Satan's idea of a messiah who had thrown himself headlong among us so as to achieve a unique and quite different prodigy – salvation. The tempter hadn't the imagination to grasp that magic worthy of a God wouldn't be changing stones into bread but bread into a body to leave for his friends; that Christ could have made that triumphal flight more usefully three years later by wrenching himself from the cross ('If you're the Son of God come down from the cross', they were to cry).

'Change stones into bread . . .' 'Throw yourself over the precipice . . .' These are the arrogant and trivial suggestions of someone who has failed to grasp things. Yet I can't detect any bitterness or contempt in the voice that answered: '*Man doesn't live by bread alone but by every word coming from the mouth of God* . . .' '*It's written: you mustn't tempt the Lord your God* . . .' Two honest, sombre reproofs, it would seem, intended to make his clumsy adversary recognize him and abandon the path of profanity and the unequal duel.

But Satan was deaf to metaphysics and continued to imagine he was dealing with someone who could be bought with the tinsel of this world; all he had to do was to raise the price. So he led him to the top of a mountain, spread the total treasure before his eyes and threw this bribe in his face: '*I'll give you all this power and the glory of these kingdoms, if you will adore me.*'

What does 'I'll give you' mean? Is Satan really capable of giving away the kingdoms of the earth; is the world really his? There was once a silly doctrine which said that only the spirit appertained to God, and matter (forests, cathedrals, rivers and gardens) belonged to the Devil. Whereas really he's a usurper, and is only master of the foaming pollution we spread over the earth: greed, avarice, tyranny, and everything that – even before it denies goodness – denies the divine poetry of the world.

'Go away, Satan', Christ now shouted. With the command that finally drove him away, Christ wasn't defending his own incorruptibility which makes a mockery of power and success; he was defending the world, the swarming valleys and seas that his eyes took in from the top of the mountain. 'Go away': Jesus shouts this even now to me when I challenge him with the temptations of the desert, when I make a superstitious bargain and offer him my heart, when I claim as mine realms that belong to him, when with philosophical stratagems I water down his quite different nature.

The primary reason why Christ let himself be tempted is this: so that in our dealings with him we shouldn't try to tempt him in the same way, we shouldn't build our faith on a mean and sickly image of him.

The evangelist says that at this point the angels came and ministered to him. Satan made off over the sandhills; and we, as we come to the end of this hazardous section, realize that the course of the temptation was the opposite of what it seemed. It was Christ who tempted the tempter to play his obtuse game. Jesus provoked the other so that he'd understand who he was, and the other didn't understand. So Satan was in the same boat as his mother had been when earlier on she rebuked him when he returned from the temple; so are we all, so am I. Faced with the mystery of Christ we're all in the dark; sinners and saints, the Devil and the Madonna.

THE MIRACLES

Do you believe I can do this?

SO THAT YOU'LL BELIEVE . . .

I know two kinds of believer. Those who need miracles to believe, and those for whom miracles don't add an ounce to faith but are even rather embarrassing.

We shouldn't laugh at the first kind; they're in good company for St Augustine said: 'Without the miracles I wouldn't be a Christian.' And we shouldn't take the second kind at their word. If I went into any Italian square at a peak hour of the traffic, or at market time, and shouted that the Madonna had appeared a mile away, I'm quite sure the square would be emptied in the wink of an eye. And the first to run might well be the materialists, the so-called unbelievers; but hard on their heels, and just as breathless, there'd be many of those friends of mine who say: 'For me a miracle is something superfluous, my faith has no need of miracles.'

The truth about all of us is no more than this: that we're miracles ourselves, that we come from miracles and are made for miracles. A miracle – for anyone privileged to witness one in the course of his life – is like returning home; nothing brings more peace to the soul of man than to see a worker fall from the fifth floor of a building and remain unhurt, nothing is more homelike than a wound that dries up in contact with a relic, or another wound that immediately opens in the hands, feet and side of a saint – because we were born there, in that land where no fifth floors exist and where the only known wounds are those of the crucified Christ.

And for human beings there's nothing more foreign, inexplicable and intolerable than nature which ties them down with its laws; the massive weight of causality that holds us unremittingly in thrall – by which a stone drops if your hand lets it fall, or the heart of a loved one stops if one of the wretched valves of that muscular machine breaks down.

It's not true that the world itself is a miracle – the rising moon, the seed that turns into a plant, the ant that hoards provisions for the winter. Those who say it is are guilty of malicious equivocation and are lying. The world is marvellous but it doesn't satisfy us. We were born for a world where ants talk, magnolia seeds give birth to gazelles, and the moon falls into a well as in the poets' metaphor.

At this moment, among all the people breathing under heaven, there isn't a single one who doesn't hanker after a miracle.

Today, more than ever before, we're dying of this thirst. Science produces a dizzy succession of prodigies and the more complicated and amazing they become the more they confirm our humiliation at being unable to perform miracles, at being restricted to clever embroidery on the network of laws by which nature ensnares us. We harness gigantic waterfalls but we can't make a drop of rain; we hear people talking about the moon but we can't hear the voices of our dead who press upon us when we think we're alone.

Every man-made miracle is enclosed and explained by some sort of cylindric bobbin in a test-tube; but in the tales of our childhood there weren't any bobbins or test-tubes: the frog turned into the handsome prince only because the fairy princess bent down to kiss him. Thus even a man who has everything longs for a miracle, because a miracle is more than a kindly act of help or a useful present or a dispensation from pain; it's the intoxication of childhood returning to bewitch us; it's the revenge of early innocent wisdom on the illusory knowledge that follows it; it's the flag of our homeland flying on foreign soil in a wasteland of days that aren't ours and depicting the castle where we were born by a miracle.

The gospel is the field of miracles. There's scarcely a day in those thousand days between Nazareth and Calvary, scarcely a page turned on which the thrill of some awesome happening doesn't pulsate through the people who recognized Jesus and made supplications to him. Yet one thing stares us in the face: that Christ was an enemy of miracles.

'O wicked and adulterous generation, you don't believe unless you see miracles . . .'

To a greater or lesser extent all his miracles were extorted from him – either dragged from his pity, snatched from his indulgence, or even stolen from him by cunning.

And every time he agreed to perform a miracle, as with the man whose eyes were opened, the cripple who threw away his crutches or the man raised from the dead, we realize that it's only for us that it's a miracle plain and simple. For him, miracles meant something else; they meant what they would subsequently produce, the thing for which he turned himself into a wizard, but only rarely got: namely, faith.

'So that you'll believe . . . I tell you, get up and take your bed . . .' 'Do you believe I can do this?' 'Yes, Lord.' 'It'll be done to you according to your faith.' 'If you can believe, everything is possible for the believer.' 'Get up and go, your faith has cured you.'

Our greed for miracles is so great that we clap our hands when the paralysed man jumps up, when the hunchbacked woman becomes straight, when the dumb man speaks or Jairus' daughter wakes up on her deathbed: perhaps we even weep with hope and consolation, but we fail to realize that for him each of these miracles left a wound in the depths of his soul because each showed that his word wasn't enough for our wretched faith.

I'll tell the story of Christ's miracles in terms of things happening to *us*, because as soon as we think of our own lives we are all at Jericho, Bethesda, Gadara, on Lake Tiberias or in the tomb at Bethany. We've experienced blindness, paralysis, insanity, storms and death. A thousand times we've been told 'ephphatha' and our tongues have been loosened, 'be cleansed' and our sores have disappeared, 'come out' and the stone of the sepulchre has opened to release us from our darkness.

The real, decisive miracle of the gospel is something quite different. It concerns two strapping men who got up and followed him without once looking back. *When he'd gone a bit further Jesus saw two men, James and John, in the boat where they were mending nets with their father Zebedee and he immediately called them. And they left the boat and their father with the fisher-boys, and followed him.*

We stayed behind mending our nets though he looked at us more than once; peaceably, from the boat with our father and the fisher-boys we spoilt the really rare miracle, the one compared with which the raising of Lazarus was no more than a game. The miracle that he succeeds in performing on one person in a thousand and which no one has ever been able to relate: following him.

THE HOUR

When the wine gave out his mother said to him: 'They've no more wine.' He answered: 'Woman, what's that to me or to you? My hour hasn't yet come.' But his mother said to the servants: 'Do everything he tells you.'

What *was* his hour? Perhaps he'd decided to begin with the cripple or at someone's bedside (Peter's mother-in-law, whose fever disappeared, was to be his second miracle). Or perhaps his hour meant any odd moment, out of doors, at a sign from the swallows, at some imperceptible stirring of the blood.

Obviously his hour was drawing near. Three days earlier on the road he'd heard the cry: *'There goes the lamb of God.'* And if he looked at someone even without opening his mouth, that person would stop mending his nets or counting money on his bench and follow him. Time, like ears of ripe corn, was offering its hours to him to choose one and begin.

This at any rate wasn't his hour. A wedding feast: plenty of greedy people who had come for amusement; a nervous girl; an impatient husband; an atmosphere, willy-nilly, of bawdy double-meanings. And the guests getting more and more drunk so that he stood out among them owing to his dreamy reserve.

His was to be another hour. But when? He kept it secret

57

like a strategist who keeps quiet about the moment when he's going to attack. It was even a secret from his mother. And the dialogue which flared up with her at table in Cana – words murmured by scarcely moving lips used to understanding one another from years at home – was a brief battle of wills.

'They've run out of wine. You and I are the only ones who know; only you and I can provide it for them. Without wine a wedding feast can become incredibly dreary. Don't let the girl start her married life with a humiliation like this. For us women these aren't small matters that can be overlooked, and the joys we most look forward to are easily spoilt. The harmony of this wedding-feast deserves a miracle.'

'What does it matter to me or you? Their hours of joy and pain are already numbered. In days to come they'll often be short of wine and I won't be there. Leave me alone, mother, to end my time of vigil in peace. Let me still linger on this side of the frontier, in this world where wine comes to an end and water remains water. Let me stay at home a little longer, I'm still only the carpenter of Nazareth: there's no life as gentle as that, having a mother, a quiet corner, and a bed to rest your head on. You ought to know what will happen to me once they know who I am, and where pity for these poor people will lead me.'

'I do know. But they haven't any wine.'

'Good-bye then, if you insist. You know what orders to give the servants and I'll do what you want without anyone noticing. We'll part here, beside that jar full of water. Soon it will be wine. One day I'll change wine too, and that will be my last miracle.'

Mary won as she'd never won before and would never win again. She looked at her son and at the revellers who were amazed to find themselves drinking vintage wine. She was happy. She would have liked her son's whole mission to stop there at the table in Cana, with that jolly subterfuge among the servants, that small triumph, because now everyone had noticed the prodigy and were queuing up to be his disciples. She didn't realize that this happening had set everything going before time. The miracle machine was turning and it was she who had chosen the hour. She had set it in motion and had no idea where it would lead him.

HIS HOME

. . . then he got into one of the boats belonging to Simon and asked him to move a little offshore.

Gennesaret – an enchanted word. This story often wanders into your waters and when I write your name I get a sense of repose and seem to be purifying my pen in your ripples. You're always in the background of Jesus' travels and words, like a net ready to gather him in. Your banks gleam behind him, they seem like a legion of angels made liquid so as to watch over him from near to, so as to protect him under a twofold vesture. And his resurrected body was once again to choose your shores for his first outdoor appearance.

So the homeless man made you his home and refuge; he had a way of getting into Peter's boat and saying to his companions: 'Move a little offshore.'

A few strokes of the oar were enough. Then they stopped at a point where the hedge of human faces left behind could still be seen, and in each face its individual need.

But the dust didn't reach the boat, nor the breath or hands or oppressive fanaticism of these people. Not that he shunned them but he sometimes seemed to show a desire to get away from them so as to find purer words, a minor transfiguration on the floating boat.

From this vantage-point the wretchedness of the people, squashed on the shore like animals who didn't dare wade out, seemed to him greater than ever; from there he could embrace them all with that greeting which remains the most sorrowful and most human of any he pronounced on earth: '*I have compassion on the masses.*'

Gennesaret: a *noli me tangere* from which he could bring goodness to people without being sullied by them. It would have been fine if he could have completed the whole work of salvation from the boat, cure people with the mere sound of his voice which the water clothed in an indescribable echo.

Looked at like this the lake offers us a truer and more secret explanation of his miracles. The extraordinary catch of fish, his sleep during the storm, the shadows stalking between the wind and the moon, that night when we too would have felt the impulse to throw ourselves overboard and run over the water barefoot, as over a meadow, towards him as he calls us and eludes us . . .

Perhaps his last glance from the mountain sought out the lake of Gennesaret down there towards Galilee; and before he went up to the Father his ghost tarried wandering over the waters.

HE WAS ASLEEP IN THE STERN

And a mighty wind blew up which drove the waves over the boat and filled it with water. They were in danger; but Jesus was asleep in the stern with his head on a pillow.

I'm not interested in big miracles – such as the lake's raging waves being appeased. What interests me is his sleeping face in the stern amidst the spray and clatter of the storm. I'm not interested in what happened outside the boat, I'm interested in what happened inside it, the conflict of instincts when the boat was in danger.

I'm interested in those men like me, with death below them and terror in their hearts; those disciples who, now that they were threatened by extinction, felt that they'd lived with Jesus, heard his parables and seen the dead raised – in vain.

And I'm interested in that man unlike me, who slept; and in the words: '*Master, don't you mind if we sink?*' '*Why are you afraid – is your faith so weak?*'

Storm in their hearts; shipwreck of the faith built up with such infinite care by the Son of man and now drowned in the waves.

Possibly this miracle is the most tragic and discouraging

of them all, and that sleeping head the most necessary and most neglected lesson of the whole book. Because Christ's religion would prefer to do without miracles; his message was wholly contained in that sleep of his at the bottom of the boat, that absurd, stubborn, boyish sleep. And our few saints are nothing but sleepers in the storm – among us panicky ones who shake them. '*Why are you afraid? Have you still no faith?* Haven't I taught you that life and death are both beautiful?'

'No, Lord. Death is ugly. One dies without friends. One goes off there alone and seems never to have known anyone, not even you.'

Men like others. They didn't want to die. They didn't want to believe. All they wanted was a miracle, the lake to be calmed and death to fade away beyond the crest of the hills.

And in fact the lake does become calm and the sky shines bright and homely. Just as we wanted it. And in the joy of being alive and safe around him, the shame of our unbelief and cowardice doesn't weigh us down one bit.

We know once and for all that his sleeping face, and the peace of his features astern on top of the pile of nets, aren't enough. A sleeping God is too like a dead God: a God who doesn't exist.

FISHES AND MEN

Then Simon answered: 'Master, we've toiled all night and haven't caught a thing; but still, if you say so I'll cast the nets.' When they had done this, Simon and Andrew his brother caught such a quantity of fish that their net broke.

From the empty net – which, after a solid night's fishing, had perhaps picked up a few dead crabs and some weed – it was a big jump to a net bursting with fish. But as good fishermen, Simon and Andrew bent over the gift before turning to the giver: over the mass of captive fish, all wriggling noses and writhing tentacles; their expert eye could tell their names and assess their value.

Simon and Andrew grappled with the bursting meshes, their veins swollen on their muscles, their eyes riveted on their catch so as to hold it back if the net accidentally broke.

Those fishes in that net! There were so many of them that if they could have formed a choir of supplication it would have re-echoed over the lake and surrounding hills. But the fish died silently, and in the brief drama of their lives there were only the jerks to shake out the water and the men's breathless 'Come on . . . heave!'

Christ was waiting for them on the shore. What with him and the groaning boat, the crowd was jubilant; but he didn't move, he didn't even want to look at the miraculous catch.

He said: *'If you follow me, I'll make you into fishers of men.'*

'Rabbi . . . Rabbi . . .' (Kneeling at his feet, Simon and Andrew were looking out of the corner of their eyes to see that no one laid hands on their booty; they were calculating its weight and multiplying it by the price of fish; trout were fetching so much, pike so much, needle-fish so much, eels so much . . .) 'Of course we'll follow you!'

Jesus had told them to get up. They'd need to hurry if they wanted to follow him. And the two brothers were ready to leave both boat and nets, but first they wanted to examine that load of fish, handle it, sort it out into baskets. They were in ecstasy. They caressed the smooth tapered bodies, calling each by its name; they examined them under the gills and against the sun, as born fishermen do.

'Fishers of men?' Simon was thinking, as he held two splendid pike in his fist. 'If they were men what would we do with them?'

You thought you were counting fish, Simon, and you were counting men. Behind your back on the beach those fish were casting human shadows. Shadows of kings and mounted warriors; of persecutors and martyrs; of prostitutes, philosophers, gladiators, beggars, idlers, murderers; torrents of men. Jesus Christ's immense catch in the sea of the centuries, right down to my father, my mother, and I who am writing – we were all struggling in your net, Simon. And you failed to see that every fish was casting a human shadow on the shore.

A GHOST

And Peter got out of the boat and walked on the water to join Jesus. But when he saw the raging wind he felt afraid, began to sink and shouted: 'Lord, save me!'

There are many threads in this nocturnal miracle. Let's try to disentangle its wonders.

Oars in the silence of the night. It was the disciples' boat. They were on their way back from Bethsaida to Capernaum. It had been a heavy day: the miracle of the loaves and fishes had happened only a few hours before. The men were still stupefied by that prodigy and by the joyful task of emptying the inexhaustible baskets. Then the Master had sent them away with the boat and gone up a mountain to pray. And in the boat they were weighed down by that vague fear that always assailed them when he wasn't there, that longing for another sort of life that made them silent and seem almost strangers to each other. At such times the fact of belonging to him didn't count. A trembling leaf, not to mention a ghost, would make them jump to their feet, their hands in their hair.

A cry: 'Look over there! A ghost . . .'

Yes, a figure was walking on the waves and the moon threw its long shadow over the lake. It was a figure without a face, just with those haunting steps directed – there could be no further doubt about it – towards the boat.

'Go away, ghost . . .'

'I'm coming to you', the steps on the water were saying. 'I was tired of praying; make room for me.'

But they still didn't recognize him, so he had to make another salutation, and cried:

'Courage, it's me; don't be frightened.'

A jump. Someone had climbed over the side of the boat and thrown himself into the water. Now two people were upright on the waves walking towards each other. It was Peter who had leapt overboard. He was the only one to leave the com-

63

panionship of his safe corner and throw himself onto the black waves of unknown depth. Why? We know why – because he loved Jesus more than the others did. But Peter also felt a personal temptation of professional curiosity. What a revenge for a fisherman to be able to walk on the water, the treacherous water . . . And Peter gave way to the intoxication of that challenge which for an instant made him like the other, held him up in the same magic way. Perhaps the kingdom of heaven consisted in walking on the water with one's feet dry and one's body as light as a seagull's.

Then a plunge. Peter sank headlong into the lake. The water suddenly opened under him and once more became the hostile beast that sucks all heavy things in. '*Lord, save me . . .*'

What had happened? Why at a certain moment did he begin to sink and throw the miracle out of gear?

Faith is an impalpable flash. Who can mark the frontier between faith and doubt? Even Peter was unaware of the imperceptible thought which made his heart beat faster and made him murmur: 'Will I make it?' But it was enough and the waters opened. Then the other one grasped his hand and set him afloat again.

'*Man of weak faith, why did you doubt?*'

PETER, A MAN LIKE ME

'*Look, we gave up everything and followed you; so what will we get?*'
   '*And are you, Lord, washing my feet?*'
'*Even if I had to die with you, I won't deny you.*'
'*I don't know that man.*'
'*Lord, you know everything, and you know that I love you.*'
'*You are blessed, Simon, son of John, because it isn't flesh and blood that revealed it to you, but my Father who is in heaven. And I tell you that you are Peter . . .*'

You, Peter, are the focus of these miracles on the lake. You're a waterman and a boatman and it's with the help of these aquatic prodigies that your portrait is filled in – sun-brown
64

against the green backcloth of the lake. These seaman's adventures give us our picture of you and that's the way it will be for thousands of years; crude lighting and shading, fixed and precise words and actions.

Your words and actions, Peter, mark your limitations. You weren't a good leader of a crew when the captain slept in the storm, nor even a good swimmer, as we can see from the night you jumped out of the boat. But it's because of these limitations that we love you; because they're ours; and we share your clumsiness and impetuosity. Your hunger for life and for miracles, your gesticulations, your fear of death, your courage in betrayal are the very things we have. Yet we've also inherited your mute dog-like devotion, your sincere tears when the cock crew, your impatience that set you running to the tomb at dawn to be among the first to see him.

Like ours, your whole story lies here, played out on those red and black squares of faith and doubt, on that flashing and fading of a lighthouse at night. Even the phrase with which he tormented you every day – '*Why did you doubt?*' – hammers also at us.

Peter, faith, Peter, faith . . . Two words swirling round in an inextricable drama. What, Peter, was that word that entered your life like a cancer, abstract and insidious as an evening breeze, falling precisely on you, a poor fisherman, accustomed to saying fish, oar, tar, to living peaceably with rough things that dirtied your hands?

With those miracles on the lake we learn everything about you, because a man is a single sin, and yours was obstinate resistance to the light and adherence to your old seaman's common sense. In a word, it lay in your very being as a man, son of contradiction and fear, capable of greatness and baseness.

That's why we love you, Peter, because you were a man. And that's why he gave you to us as a leader, poor bastard like the rest of us.

To call you our leader we don't have to think of you being crucified upside down. It's enough that you jumped out of the boat that night on Lake Tiberias.

FIVE AND TWO MAKE A HUNDRED
THOUSAND

And he divided the two fish among everybody and had as much given to them as they wanted. All ate and were satisfied.

THE FISH: We're the fish of the miracle. We weren't born in the depths of the sea, in the caves where the water is jade-coloured and the sand very fine, and we never swam.

We were born in the disciples' baskets and our silver scales shone in the air. We were stillborn, but our momentary life was far more wonderful than that of our free and living brothers and sisters.

The hands of Peter and Philip and Andrew collected us from the bottom of the basket and suddenly another of us, seven, twenty others were born in the place left vacant. If you opened us you found that we had backbones and gills like other fish, but we'd never been in the sea, we had no father or mother – only that potent command that fished us out of that other motionless and empty sea, the sea called nothingness.

From nothingness we were thrown up into charity, and suddenly we confronted the short but essential task of all that exists – that of giving ourselves.

We were born in that immediacy; while the disciple turned his head to give us to the hungry – that crowd of 5,000 men, women and children who didn't want to go away but wanted to go on listening to Jesus. We laughed with our bulging eyes at your human amazement, at your belief that fish are born in the sea, in a lake or in the breeding-ground of a river merely because that's what you'd always been taught.

We may be born near someone who is hungrier for truth than for our succulent flesh. You try to catch us and we dart away in a flash, but we can also leave the sea and offer ourselves to you in a meadow when you've lived with him for three days and have forgotten to eat.

66

'Pick up the remains so that nothing's wasted.' They picked them up; and filled twelve baskets with pieces of bread.

THE LOAVES: We too – we hadn't ears of corn as our mothers, we never felt the scythe, the thudding of the threshing-floor, the grinding of the mill, the kneading by the happy baker late at night and the roar of the oven that raises the leaven inside us.

But here, have a look, and you'll still see our remains in the twelve baskets. We were bread, real bread for hunger, just like all the anonymous bread in the world. And those who munched us didn't notice us because hunger is beyond noticing miracles. We alone knew how we were born; we alone knew who pushed up our golden forms in response to a thousand outstretched hands; and we remember the moment when, all unseen, we took cunning consistency in dozens beneath the overflowing heap.

Our baker never dipped his hands in flour. All he said was: *'There's no need for them to go away. Make the people sit down on the grass.'* It was enough to say that. It was enough not to send the hungry away, and the bread was made.

There's a piece of bread travelling through the world that no one has yet succeeded in finishing, and the more you eat the more it accumulates: we are the crumbs of Bethsaida, we, the five cold yellow loaves harvested from the apostles' haversacks. When you are asked for something you think you're unable to give remember us, the pieces of bread left over in the twelve baskets.

GOD'S ANGER

. . . but when they approached and saw nothing there but leaves, because it wasn't the season for figs, Jesus said to the fig-tree: 'For all eternity may no one eat your fruit again!' And the tree immediately dried up.

MATTHEW: We were walking peacefully through the fields as happens on certain spring mornings.

JAMES: A lovely day. We were glad he wasn't talking and we weren't talking either. We were walking with a bit of a gap between each of us. We would have liked to have gone on like that till evening, thinking over the memories of distant years which the April breeze brought back to us.

ANDREW: He was just ahead of us and his red tunic looked like a flag between the vine-rows and the hedges.

PHILIP: It was fine for once to follow him through the fields without sick people asking us to cure them, without doctors asking us questions about the law and without his difficult parables.

JUDE: Here there was an olive tree, here a milk-vetch, here a mulberry bush. The Master stopped at every tree and the file of us disciples gathered in a group behind him and we looked at the trees one by one. Then, when the Master moved on, we went on too, separating, each with his own thoughts.

THOMAS: Then he came to the fig-tree. I thought it was a splendid fig-tree, and I was thinking of all the lovely figs that would have been born from those flowers by October . . . I could savour their delicious taste in my mouth. Then suddenly there was a shout . . .

JAMES THE LESS: The shout didn't sound at all like his voice but like a word uttered above the clouds by someone who hadn't a mouth; and it travelled across the countryside like a fiery horse. Afterwards I said to myself: 'All's over.'

BARTHOLOMEW: I said 'All's over' too. And I realized that within five days it would be the sabbath and Passover. And we were all counting a lot on that Passover (now that the people honoured him and only the day before had greeted him with waving palms). We hoped it would be a peaceful supper with all thirteen of us at table around the Lamb.

JOHN: The day before had been a fine festival. Passover and the solemn feast of the Azymes were drawing near. That day I was feeling happy because nothing extraordinary had happened and I hoped that when the sun set things would still be that way – for once giving us a pause to taste the joy of living together. But then I saw that we have no days off. And this was

68

the worst day we'd had since we began living with him. We'd never seen him like that . . .

SIMON THE ZEALOT: Never. He had thundered against Jerusalem, he had inveighed against the Pharisees with insulting words, he had driven the sellers out of the temple. But he'd never destroyed anything. He might raise his hand in a threat but he never struck. And now he swooped and did strike: he killed a fig-tree, a poor wooden fig-tree. Why?

PETER: Who'll ever forget that tree . . . Our eyes had seen lepers, the faces of people possessed by the Devil, people who'd been dead for four days: but that withered tree in the middle of the fields darkened my eyes as nothing else has done since I was born.

Come on, one of you others, say something. Say what you think, set us free from this nightmare because I don't understand, the ground has slipped from under my feet and perhaps we've taken the wrong path . . .

JUDAS: You're making too much of what happened. We know that this isn't the season for figs. Fig-trees ripen in the autumn when the leaves fall and the marmot goes back to its lair. All that happened was that the Master forgot this. His mind is always lost in higher thoughts far away from us and the small matters of here below . . . As I see things it's all very simple and that's all there is to it. Even he can make a mistake for once because he's a man like us. So calm down. And don't despair because there's one tree less.

THE SICK IN PUBLIC PLACES

Wherever he entered, in villages, cottages or cities, they laid down the sick in the open and prayed to be allowed at least to touch the hem of his tunic; and everyone who touched him was cured.

Everyone who touched him . . . So numbers, vast numbers, a countless mass.

And yet, those who do not experience these miracles as the mysterious sign put forward by Christ can be scandalized by them, fall into a rage and give up their faith; they listen to these stories of marvels with sarcastic or derisive laughter. Why are the many in fact so few? Why is it 'no' for the millions and 'yes' for the handful? From the depths of his bed the incurable man in hospital may accuse a Christ who was only concerned with people near him, those born in his tiny corner of history; and accuse me for writing Christ's story.

I, too, am tempted to react in this way. I, too, don't know why that tiny portion of health and happiness restored should float like a cork in the sea of human suffering. On such occasions I say that the value of those odd hundreds of cures is symbolic, a metaphor for all the others, for those excluded and left in their agony. So as to teach them that at least they mustn't lose the health of faith (after all Jesus cured so as to strengthen that faith); so that they may realize that Christ would like to see them healed and happy too, and that were he on earth he would certainly touch them; so that his desire, his longing to be able to cure them, should be a common medicine for everyone. I don't know. At any rate I know that sickness and health are not our affair. I know that any morning we may wake up, stretch our lithe and voluptuous limbs, and not know whether, when we stand up, we won't find our legs crippled with paralysis, or, if we go to the mirror, we won't see on our faces the sign of some terrible disease that came to a head during the night. It's an immense paradox, but man is only master of his own soul; if he wants to, he can save it, if he doesn't want to, he can lose it. But he isn't master of his own physical health, of his body in which his blood circulates second by second, of the network of his nerves, of the solid yet extremely fragile scaffolding of his bones. Someone else is the master of all that. Perhaps the person with whom man allied himself against the Father, man's ancient enemy who, from his sinister observatory, administers the physical pains of the world, tirelessly studies and multiplies illnesses, and says to each individual: 'Here's your pain for you: suffer.'

I know that as he passed through the streets Christ waged a relentless war against this mysterious murderer. He used his hands and his voice from the hour he got up in the morning till the lights of the city went out: he invented the miracle.

Beds, stretchers, straw mattresses; the festering bandages of lepers, the fire of fever and the ice of paralysis; the yelping of deaf-mutes and the red and white eyes of the blind. All the human misery of bodies was there, packed tight and groaning around him, incredulous or imploring but never resigned to suffering.

Possibly some of them were to be among the first martyrs and were to endure scourging and death without a murmur; but they couldn't endure illness.

So Christ confronted man's great fear. He almost always performed his miracles in a material way by touching people with his hands or his saliva, or breathing on them. And he only granted miracles with his mind and from a distance on two pagans (the woman from Canaan and the Roman) because of their faith – which was greater than that of Israel.

So when Jesus passed by it became a festival of joy and Job's lament was placated. It became God's happiness shown in its most homely form. The doctor-redeemer who knew that to human creatures, whether in miserable poverty or in high places, it's easier to say: 'Go to the firing-squad' than 'endure your illness'.

We could say that any miracle that isn't a spiritual conversion is superfluous. But in that case the gospel is loaded with superfluous miracles: precisely because he came to make the Law human and remind men of gentleness and mercy – which is alive and can be detected even in the Old Testament, but was hidden and forgotten: '*I prefer mercy to sacrifice.*'

THE THEFT

At that very moment the flow of blood was stanched and she felt she was cured. Jesus was aware that virtue had gone out of him and turned to the crowd and asked: 'Who touched my tunic?'

Of all the cures, this one may well be the best for explaining the mechanism of a miracle, of this happening between ourselves and God.

Jesus was wearing a tunic. We hadn't the courage to touch his body and we didn't dare meet his eyes. But covering his body there was this linen tunic which is earthly matter woven on our looms, and we might be able to touch it, without his noticing, if we stretched out our hands.

There were favours we felt ashamed to ask for, sores we had too much pride to show even to have them cured. The woman the book talks of, who was scared by the crowd, was suffering from a haemorrhage. Luke, who was a doctor, hints at a history of persistent efforts and sacrifices: *For twelve years she had suffered from loss of blood and had spent all her money on doctors but nobody could cure her*. Now here she was after all these years, penniless and disillusioned; all she had was that obstinate flow of blood that had never stopped, would never stop, seeping from her body. But there was a tunic there, swinging from side to side in that concourse of people, though in her unhinged and delicate condition it seemed absurd to try to get through that wall of backs that wouldn't make way, and all that cursing and shoving. But the poor sick woman managed it; she pushed her way through and finally arrived at the back of that tunic and just managed to reach it.

'*Who touched me?*'

An unreasonable question. Peter lost his patience and protested: '*Master, people are thronging round you and pressing against you and now you ask "Who touched me?"*'

Lord, we all touch you when we think no one's looking. All of us are suffering from some deep-seated illness that the doctors here below can't heal. An ugly illness that we're ashamed to name. For such cases there's the tunic full of unguarded miracles – the thing you'd forgotten you were wearing. If you turn to see who stole the miracle from you, you'll find an enterprising little old woman prostrate at your feet, feeling like a thief with the extra shame of having to own up. She'd like to thrust back into your tunic what she's taken from you. So you had to explain that it wasn't the tunic, it wasn't a theft, that the merit wasn't even yours but came from something else: *'Cheer up, my daughter; it is your faith that has saved you.'*

THE MIRACLES ON THE SABBATH

The scribes and Pharisees kept a watch over him to see if he would cure people on the sabbath.

So we come to the sabbath miracles; for us dark, dark miracles that plumb the very depths of our vileness.

The man with dropsy, the hunchbacked woman, the man with the withered hand, the paralytic at Capernaum – all of them spread a black truth throughout the world: that when Jesus cured them after their years of torment, the other people, the healthy people, were shocked and exclaimed, 'But it's the sabbath!'

So each of these cured people had two miracles to relate, the miracle of the Father's pity and the equally amazing miracle of their brothers' hard-heartedness. In their memories the two went together: Christ's happy regard, and the sullen stare of the onlookers; his voice saying 'Go in peace', and the snarl of the jackals tied down to the petty precept, 'It's the sabbath'.

I don't envy the people on whom those miracles were worked. I don't know which of those twin miracles would have affected their destiny most. I don't know whether they'd have been able to save their souls, whether after that particular sabbath they'd have managed to love (besides God) that fiend called their neighbour.

THE WITHERED HAND

Then, when he'd glanced around, he told the man: 'Stretch out your hand.' He stretched it out and the hand became healthy again like the other. But the Pharisees were enraged and talked among themselves about how to rid the world of him.

To bring a hand back to life is rather like bringing a person

73

back to life because the hand has a soul; the hand lives –
alongside the man who possesses it – its own little thoughtful
and mysterious life.

Man's hand can sweep away an island from the sea, make a
plain where there was a mountain, fill a desert with towers
or tulips; but it can do even more irreplaceable things: when,
owing to distance, we can no longer see the face of someone
we're leaving, only his hand can still say to us: 'Good-bye,
come back soon!'

When a man performs an action, his eyes, ears and even his
tongue obey him, they do what they're told. Whereas with a
hand it isn't always like that. A hand is capable of good and
evil, as it were, by itself. Quick and furtive, it can precede
the thought guiding it, or else rebel and delay. It can sin or do
good on its own account. The hand of someone who thought
he was honest can stretch out for someone else's jewellery;
a hermit's hand may feel about in sleep for a woman's breast;
a murderer's hand may surprise its master by stroking a baby's
head or the back of a stray dog.

In the synagogue Jesus brought a hand back to life. According to Luke it was withered. But withered doesn't mean
dead. And Christ's story is full of withered things that bourgeon
anew. The Samaritan woman by the well in Sychar was
withered; Peter was withered on the night of his denial; the
thief crucified to the right of the cross was withered; and so
was the hand held out on the day Jesus said: 'Stretch out
your hand.'

He stretched it out; and other hands, healthy and angry
hands, pointed their forefingers: '*Is it lawful to heal on the
sabbath?*' Then those hands clasped each other in a pact of
revenge: 'We'll get him killed.' Those hands were at work too.
And on the sabbath that wasn't lawful.

WITHOUT A MAN

Now in Jerusalem, near the Sheep Gate, there was a pool called in Hebrew Bethesda, with five porticoes under which lay a large number of people, the infirm, the blind, the lame, the paralysed, who were waiting for the waters to move.

But in all this concourse our attention is drawn to one only. His head was bowed and he didn't move. Who was he?

There was a man who'd been ill for thirty-eight years.

What more can we say about him once we know this about him? What is there to say about such a man apart from the number of years? He'd been ill for thirty-eight years. We'd better count slowly from one to thirty-eight if we want to know him better.

At certain times the angel of the Lord came down into the pool and troubled the waters. Then the first person to throw himself into the pool after the water had been troubled was cured . . .

I think this angel must have been blind. For up and down he went troubling the water while Thirty-Eight stayed put, always ill. Obviously the angel didn't see Thirty-Eight, otherwise he himself would have thrown him first into the water.

When Jesus saw him lying there and knew that he'd been there for such a long time, he said to him: 'Do you want to be cured?'

Jesus was afraid that he'd stopped wanting to be cured, that he'd forgotten what health was, or why he was still quietly waiting there. Sometimes, if too long delayed, a favour frightens people when it comes. But it wasn't like that with him; he was still hoping . . .

'Lord, I haven't a man to put me in the pool as soon as the water is troubled, and by the time I get moving someone else is always ahead of me.'

He hadn't a man. Was there anyone poorer than him?

75

There were poor people without shoes, there were poor people without friends, or even a dog to lick their wounds; but was there anyone without a man, without someone to give him a good push into the water and then go away about his business? This man had been begging for a push for over thirty-eight years and no one had given him one. There he was, the man without a man. Watch how he crawls towards the water like a snake . . . come on, only another yard . . . too late: once again someone has got there first.

'Get up, take your mattress and walk.'
At last Thirty-Eight had a man. A patient voice that was entirely for him. But what did he say? He told you to get up: you're cured! But, poor wretch, your joy so blinds you that you won't be in time to see him. Your man has already disappeared into the crowd.

However, that day was the sabbath. Therefore the Jews said to the man who'd been cured: 'It's the sabbath and you can't take away that mattress of yours.'
How wretched we are. Wretched and accursed because we have eyes and hands like these people, because like these people we've sucked a woman's milk. Tell us that ours isn't the human race. They withhold his mattress, spread it out for him to lie on again . . . We say to you: 'Bite their hands.' The man who cured you would tell you to forgive even them. But we say to you: 'Bite their hands.'

THIS ISN'T WHAT WE WANT

'Which is easier, to say to a paralysed man: "Your sins have been forgiven", or to say to him: "Get up, take your mattress and walk"?'

When in an unexpectedly harsh voice Jesus presented his challenge – 'Which is easier?' – a stony silence must have spread among his listeners; one of those panic-swollen silences to be found only in the gospel (*'Let anyone who hasn't sinned*

76

throw the first stone at her'; or when he was seized in the garden: *As soon as he said 'That's me' they backed away and fell to the ground*). Pauses; silent beats that the narrator can't indicate with his pen because he isn't a musician. So they elude us too; but if we could bring their charge to life we would tremble like those people swarming round the paralysed man at Capernaum.

On this occasion the scene was indoors, in a house. There had recently been long disputes about doctrine (imposed on the Master by a number of learned faces come from as far away as Jerusalem to keep watch on him). But suddenly, owing to popular impatience, the roof was uncovered and without any learned preambles the people lowered down the most concrete and urgent thing that exists: a man in pain. That swinging burden put a stop to wordy eloquence and turned it into another kind of eloquence: that of a stretcher, a few rags, unwholesome flesh, and two speaking eyes. And Jesus immediately granted the gift: '*Son, your sins are forgiven you.*'

But where was the rejoicing for this huge favour? The Master looked around and saw lowered eyes, disappointed faces. And very legible in those faces were the words of thanks: 'This man hasn't understood. We went to all the trouble of opening the roof only to find that he forgave sins . . .'

'He hasn't understood. I'd hoped to be running along the garden path this evening . . .'

No, we don't want this kind of gift. We want to run on sound legs, to eat if we're hungry, drink if we're thirsty, save ourselves in a sinking boat, see, feel, touch, and live a long life. This is why we come to look for you and why, if needs be, we uncover roofs. If you give us back our innocence and our peace of heart, all we do is mutter: 'Is that all?'

In vain Jesus looked for a sign of joy on those faces; but there was only the malicious satisfaction of the group of Pharisees. God alone could forgive sins. Today that man had blasphemed and they had caught him in the act . . .

'But tell me', Jesus cried, 'which is easier?' No one answered. And we would all be like that today, we'd be mute in that house in Capernaum. And so as not to make our baseness last

77

for ever, he again broke the silence, this time to ordain a miracle: *'Get up and walk.'*

Then everyone was happy. The rabbi from Nazareth was a god. That evening the cripple would run along the garden path and everyone would dance. But one man went off alone. And took the road to the mountain so as to be with the Father.

WHO'S GOING HOME?

He drew him aside, away from the crowd, put his fingers in his ears and touched his tongue with saliva. Then he raised his eyes to heaven, sighed and said: 'Ephphatha', which means 'Open'. And immediately his ears were opened and he ceased to be tongue-tied and started talking.

He drew him aside, away from the crowd.

When he could, he preferred things that way: tête-à-tête miracles which left no trace.

There were polemical miracles, successes that he needed to throw in the face of imposters and sophists. In that case, up you get, paralysed man; and all you people, watch: is it easier to forgive sins or send this man home carrying his mattress? Such miracles were bound to be spectacular, performed for the big crowds, such as the multiplication of the loaves and fishes; or triumphal, such as calming the storm or raising Lazarus, and needing the presence of a frightened human chorus.

But when possible he preferred things the other way: he preferred to take some unfortunate by the hand and lead him away along a deserted path where the gift wouldn't be dulled by the cheers and curiosity of strangers. *He took the blind man by the hand and led him out of the village* . . . Rustic corners, between trees and clouds, where he too found his rare joys on earth and could savour them with brief rapture. And then always afterwards (as with the leper and the blind man) came the anxious injunction – almost a threat – not to talk about what had happened. *'Mind you say nothing to anybody'*, *'Go home and if you have to go into the village don't talk about it to anyone.'*

'I can see . . .' 'I can talk . . .' 'I can walk . . .' 'I'm cured . . .'

Lord, who could go quietly home on such a day? Do you think there's a man in existence who'd be able to keep such good news to himself without bursting? Don't you realize that after you'd left them, their joy fell like an avalanche on the first person they met? That those houses down there were their home, their kitchen and their terrace, their chairs and their friends who knew everything about them? Do you think that for us there's anything stronger than joy, and any joys stronger than those we can share with others?

You and us – always at loggerheads. 'Ephphatha: now you can hear. You can hear the skylark in the leaves, the rattling of the pulley in the well, the woodman's axe on the tree-trunks, the wind, the hitherto unknown voice of your woman. But don't listen to anyone who asks you questions.' 'Ephphatha: now you can talk. But don't talk about this to anyone.'

So the dumb man disobeyed you too. (*But the more he forbade it*, says Mark, *the more they spread the news*.) He immediately used the tongue you had given him to betray you. And the happy hour was already smirched with disloyalty.

A CROSSROADS

'What do you want me to do for you?' He answered: 'Lord, that our eyes may be opened.' Moved by compassion, Jesus touched their eyes.

Like human shrubs beside the road, the two blind men were waiting.

Perhaps no one had told them that a miraculous prophet was going to come along from the crossroads; but blind men know even when an ant is climbing over a blade of grass. The two had sensed his arrival as a parched tree senses a cloud forming over a hill. And arm in arm, looking at the sky, they began to cry out.

Who was making that din? Shut up! The crowd was following Jesus with the self-centred zeal of courtiers, and wanted to send them packing. The Master had more to do than bother with the importunities of two beggars. He'd come to free the people of Israel, to give them dominion over all the nations, and this early morning walk following in his footsteps had gone to their heads, it smacked of setting off for the great conquest.

'Have pity on us, have pity on us . . .' They threw out their voices like a tentacle, with the despair of someone locked up who bangs for the door to be opened. '*What do you want me to do for you?*'

From the odour the two knew precisely how far Jesus was from them. From the sound of his voice, even though the question was absurd, they knew that remittance had been obtained.

'What do you want? . . .' What did he expect them to say? We have been given eyes so as not to bump our heads against a tree, so as to be able to choose the woman who delights us and look on the children she gives us. But every time he seemed to be wanting some other request – one that nobody ever made; he offered a different miracle and they didn't know what to do with it.

But soon he abandoned his weary joke, and before the two could answer he had already stretched out his hands.

He could have healed them standing still, he only had to raise his eyes to heaven. But it is written that *he touched their eyes*.

He wanted to feel those eye-sockets with his finger, to reward them for their long darkness. He delayed with his hands till he could feel them moistened by a rare drop of water: the tear of a blind man who sees.

AN OBSTINATE MAN

'*I don't know whether he's a sinner; I only know one thing: that before I was blind, and now I can see.*'

THE PHARISEES: Let's summon him a third time and start

putting an end to this imposture. But we mustn't frighten him; we must talk trustfully and persuasively.

Listen to us, friend.

THE MAN BORN BLIND: My mother's still beautiful. Until today, whenever I touched her face I felt a few wrinkles, but seeing her is another matter and I'm proud of her. Perhaps it's the colour of her eyes which are like lovely bright cornel berries, or perhaps her joy at my cure has made her young again.

THE PHARISEES: Listen to us. We're speaking for your good and we know what we're talking about. The stranger who put mud on your eyes is a common sinner . . .

THE MAN BORN BLIND: I like the colour of mud, too. When I was blind they told me it was an ugly despicable colour, whereas it was the first thing that met my eyes and it seemed to be shining like silver dust. When you see it, mud has lovely speckles and reflections.

THE PHARISEES: As we were saying, that fellow is a common sinner. We've often seen him eating with publicans, revellers and other wicked people. He talks to Samaritans and has shameless conversations with prostitutes.

THE MAN BORN BLIND: I saw a prostitute this morning for the first time. I imagined they were beautiful and bewitching. This one was wearing a shawl with blue and purple flowers, vivid colours, and round her neck she had a necklace of gold coins; but her face was wan and covered with wrinkles and she didn't arouse my senses. It's much nicer to see a bunch of grapes.

THE PHARISEES: . . . and in addition his disciples don't observe the fasts, but eat and drink. Now follow our reasoning. Today's the sabbath, isn't it? And doesn't Moses lay down that we should abstain from all activities on this day because it's dedicated to God? So how can this man who doesn't keep the sabbath come from God? Can a sinner perform prodigies like this? Come on, answer us.

THE MAN BORN BLIND: Look over there in that crack in the wall. That's a lizard. I recognize it because when I was a child I held one in my hands – my mother caught it so that,

though I was blind, I should learn what was what. Its throat
throbbed against my fingers and my mother told me they have
quick forked tongues. But I didn't know they were such a
lovely green. I thought they were black or white all over.

THE PHARISEES: You're being sly and obstinate. Watch out,
because it doesn't help a young man to set himself against us.
Whereas you stand every chance of gain if you keep on good
terms with the heads of the synagogue. For the last time, just
listen to us. It isn't true that you can see. It's all an illusion and
we've proved it to you. We know he's a sinner and a sinner
can't work miracles. Come a little closer: we want to talk to
you quietly, as real friends. You'll shut your eyes and keep them
shut because you're a blind man and blind men can't see. Have
you got the point? You can't see us . . . And the prophet of
Nazareth is an imposter. You get back to your darkness, young
man. The world is full of vile spectacles and lucky is the man
who can do without looking at them. Of course we'll make it
up to you . . .

THE MAN BORN BLIND: But what's the matter with all you
people? I see your faces changing colour: your skin has
become red, green, yellow, and your features grim and rapa-
cious. You look like birds or dogs or snakes. I haven't yet
seen men like you – my mother hadn't warned me about such
things. When I look at you a strange fear gets hold of me.

A LITTLE SALIVA

*. . . when he'd put a little saliva on his eyes and laid his hands on him
he asked him if he saw anything. The man raised his eyes and said:
'I see people walking about like trees.'*

You didn't know that the world was contained in a bit of
saliva – like a fairy-tale of a hundred thousand colours. You
were blind from birth and you pictured things around you as
they really were. On countless occasions you'd felt a man, or
you'd felt a tree, and you could have drawn them better than
someone who sees. But after the miracle your seeing was quite

different from our common eyesight. With that saliva Jesus gave you another sort of vision to make up for all your time of darkness: the legendary vision of poets who see things in an extraordinarily different way from how they appear, all mixed up in the oddest relationships.

You immediately said: 'I see people walking about like trees.'

People . . . trees . . . In a picture-book of visible things, such as an illustrated ABC, men and trees are in fact characters elementary to eyesight, they can symbolize and sum up all reality. But the miracle lay in the fact that you blended them into a single thing.

Sometimes we, too, see things that way. Lovers say: 'Look at that cloud – don't you think it looks like a cab? It is a cab! Now it's shifting and becoming an ox sitting down. And soon, if the wind swells it, it'll be a whale.'

But in our dull everyday eyesight we see men as men and trees as trees. Our eyesight is cold and slack. Whereas you, lucky blind man of the gospel, are in the right. Men are trees that walk. They have leaves, branches, nests in their hair, and yield fruit, often none too ripe. And trees are men: oaks, cypresses and birches are wise silent men, resigned to the beating of the wind and the sun.

You were given the right kind of eyesight. To us, who are incurably blind, men seem men and trees trees, and the moon and stones and cyclamen we call moon and stones and cyclamen. And more often than not we don't even look at them.

THE MASTERPIECE

So Satan invented evil and, within evil, the cruel diseases of the body.

But among the countless illnesses he devised, he thought out one that would be his masterpiece. And he unleashed his imagination to the furthest metaphysical bounds of hatred so that man should suffer something unspeakable. In his cave, like some ancient magician, he decomposed man's body, tissues, fibres and all; he examined every nerve, scrutinized bones and marrow so that not a single cell should be spared from torment and the victim's pain should reach delirious heights. But, being artful and far-sighted, he made exact and complicated calculations of anatomy and physiology so that the body would remain alive under this torment for a very long time; and the disease wouldn't lose in duration what it gained in intensity, but would be as tenacious as it was terrible, so as to hold out for years and years without the victim collapsing and being set free by death or madness. For death is a veritable festival, and madness a pleasure-garden, compared with what Satan invented that day.

Satan wanted man in all active awareness to see himself, day in and day out, covered with scabs and sores; to feel his bones pierced by spears, hacked into pieces by saws and gnawed by invisible dogs; to see filthy pus excreting from his skin, and be aware of the stink. He wanted him to fear nightfall like an accursed furnace in which, through hours like centuries, he would toss and twist till dawn; to see his fingers drop off one by one like leaves, then his ears, his nostrils and his chin – whereas his eyes would come last of all so that he could witness his own death. In a word Satan wanted to transplant a fringe of his own hell into our land of the living, and he brought among us the outlandish deathmasks of his kingdom of damnation.

Such was his masterpiece, known as leprosy.

The gospel teems with lepers. Their cry: 'Keep away, we're unclean', rang out to paralyse one's heart through the blank stretches of Palestine, amid Christ's parables, the disciples' questions and the silence of Lake Tiberias; more paralysing even than the hammering at the crucifixion. And their scabby, squinting, pocked faces wandered about in the background like strange outlawed ghosts, even stranger and more outlawed than those possessed by the Devil – so that even we, after 2,000 years, feel an instinct of repulsion and flight, like the most humane of the disciples.

No one went near them. Within a radius of several yards from their sores, all pity died.

IF YOU WANT TO . . .

A leper came to entreat him . . .

Everyone had fled. Only Jesus stayed behind. The leper was on his knees in front of him, the leper was talking. When a man is brought so low that he's nothing but a mass of suffering, his mouth only moves to say essential words. There's no cunning left, just the mournful eloquence of pain; it's impossible even to mimic entreaties with a face that's no more than a sponge, and the leper's argumentation was restricted to nine words: '*If you want to, you can make me clean.*'

If you want to. From the crest of that instant there were alternative slopes for him. A miracle, a leap into life, a house, himself and all good things; or else remaining as he was with all the ills on earth transfixing him until the last day.

'*I do want to; be clean.*'

Not a leaf stirred between these two phrases; beasts and men stood still. Only Christ's hand moved, stretched out, completed its short journey, in that span of air, from fear to pity: *he stretched out his hand and touched him . . .*

A MISSED APPOINTMENT

'*Ten were cured; and where are the nine?*'

When Jesus asked this question of the only cured leper who had kept the appointment, the man didn't answer. Prostrate at his feet, he trembled with confusion and felt that being *the only one* was embarrassing in the same way as being naked. 'Lord, how can I know? I was only a stranger among those ten. Lepers don't have names and now that you've cured their leprosy I wouldn't even be able to recognize their faces. We scattered like fish thrown back into the sea. Each went off into his own whirlpool of happiness.'

. . . *where are the nine?* Christ was waiting. This time his silence seemed stubborn, as though he were determined to wait.

Over the square there hung one of the longest pauses in the gospel. Hadn't ten been cured? The others would surely turn up too; it was impossible that they would miss the appointment; best wait for them.

Why was the silence so endless? Jesus was calling out the names of the absentees one by one and to each he repeated his question: 'Where are you?'

THE TIPPLERS: We're at the inn. We're drinking honey and fig-wine to the health of a prophet who cured us of leprosy. By chance three of us met again here, though we found it difficult to recognize each other because our faces have completely changed and the lighting in the inn is weak. But all the wine we gulped down loosened our tongues and when we discovered our miraculous fellowship we embraced and ordered more wine and began singing and making merry. What do you expect, Lord? That we should come to you? Oh, but our legs are unsteady and we've got a buzzing in our ears and we'd never be able to find the road where, this morning, you . . . By Abraham, that really was a miracle! Here's some wine, Lord, we'll drink to your health and ours . . .

THE LECHER: Here I am in a discreet corner. I ran here the moment I felt my body was as smooth as a date beneath my rags, and my mouth fresh and round where previously it gaped, and fingers were sprouting on my scabby hands. I ran to the house I knew. When I found it shut – it was early morning – I hammered at the door with my fists and shouted the woman's name. Another woman was living there instead and I had to promise her a lot of money if she'd open up and let me in, for she didn't know me and I was in rags. I plunged my hands into her warm breasts and chewed her hair. I'd done nothing but think of that sensation during all my black years of leprosy, there in my prison of sores. Crouching on

the flints of the street I'd followed with my putrid eyes the
ankles of all the women who passed and then rushed away in
horror. Now a woman's going round the room burning aloes
and soon she'll come back and lie beside me, as lovely as an
island, and the blood in my veins will turn to honey. You're
calling me, Lord, but a single hair of her head would hold me
captive more than a hundred iron chains. Anyway, Lord,
when you gave me back my mouth, my hands and my body,
what was it for but this?

THE THIEF: This thicket is a convenient hiding-place. I
can watch the landlord's movements from a distance and see
when he leaves. It won't be long. I know his habits; I carefully
registered them years ago, before I was stricken with leprosy,
and he isn't one for changing. He ought to be going out soon
to go and inspect his farm. During all that time of accursed
inertia I kept thinking of this moment and I made foolproof
plans. And during all that time the money in his safe must have
increased quite a bit. The dogs haven't heard me. And I'll
get in with a jump now that my limbs are agile and my fingers
nimble.

THE BUSINESSMAN: My good friend, this ox isn't worth
more than twenty pieces of silver. You can see for yourself
how low-haunched and short-necked it is. Twenty pieces and
not a cent more. A peasant put twenty-two pieces at my dis-
posal and don't you expect me to make a profit of at least two?
Well then, twenty-one, and if I'm not giving you a good price
may Moses strike me with leprosy. I swear by the prophets
that I wouldn't pay more even for an ox from the Nile. Oh
how pig-headed you are, you're wasting my time. See here,
friend, I've an appointment with a foreign rabbi who's expec-
ting me, and this very morning he did me a good turn without asking me for a penny. Very well, you obstinate son of
Abraham, I'll give you twenty-two. Even that won't do?
Listen . . .

THE PROUD MAN: I don't know who you are, you who are
calling me. Yes, that's my name, only you forgot to add my
title as doctor of law, and the royal line I descend from. I'm
not going out at this hour to leave my house and servants and

87

pupils. Anyone who wants to see me and needs some favour or benefit had better present himself to my scribe and wait his turn with everyone else. He can come here to my mansion, for everyone in town knows where it is. I myself don't go out because – thanks to the advantages God gave me – I've never needed anyone.

THE FORGETFUL ONE: I followed my legs just where they took me, and found myself at the top of this hill. How pure the air is! I met men and women carrying bundles of hay on their backs, a goat or two, and a sheep-dog. Yesterday even the animals fled from me in terror, whereas today they're quite tame and come up to me, and the people greet me too. I found this haystack, and when I'd watched the clouds entangled with the olive trees for a while, I fell asleep. I dreamt that I was still a leper – perhaps because the hay was pricking my skin. I woke up for a second, felt my face and hands, then closed my eyes again.

THE LOVER: Lord, I didn't forget your appointment. But I'm ill again. I caught the leprosy you took away immediately afterwards, when she kissed me, and now I've gone back to living with her in our lepers' den. As you know, I fell in love with her that day at the well. She was bending over a bucket drinking and I treacherously kissed her neck. She didn't know about my illness and she couldn't see it on my body, so she kissed me back, then came to live with me and caught the infection. Day by day our love grew with our sores. Lord, I'm not ashamed and I don't repent. It was only by chance that I was among the ten this morning and for a moment I, too, caught their obsession about being cured. But the moment your hand touched me I realized I'd lost her. So I ran back to her and wanted her to kiss me as I'd kissed her by the well. So I'm a leper again. You wasted a miracle on me and I can't come to your appointment.

The tenth leper is still there with his lips to the rock. But we other lepers are bustling about in the world. The minute he cured us we took up our life again at the precise point where it had been interrupted.

88

One in ten, Lord; that's our percentage. Don't waste miracles on us.

THE OTHER INCARNATION

But there's an affliction even worse than leprosy and it's just called Satan. People call it madness because they've lost all sense of first causes, but the gospel, which speaks in concrete terms, goes straight to the protagonists: *As soon as Judas had taken the mouthful of bread, Satan entered into him.*

What do we know about Satan or of his tragic exile? It's certain that Satan falls in love with some of us and entwines himself with our breath in a fierce embrace.

Thus Satan enters man. Man is a castle of flesh and dreams, he is beautiful and has the aroma of a lamb: man is God's territory. It's one thing to draw near him so as to tempt and corrupt him: it's another to dwell within him, to feel the jar he puts to his lips, the longing for sex that rises from his genitals, the bell of his heart tolling in the mystery of human time.

Satan is jealous of Christ and has imitated him as best he can. So there exists Christ's incarnation and there also exists an incarnation specific to Satan. These are those 'possessed by the Devil', and the book shows us various examples of them.

FACE TO FACE

They were always there at night among the tombs and on the hills shouting and fighting with stones, and they were so enraged that no one could go near them.

We never sleep. At night we lean over the crags to see our faces mirrored in the dark pools of the valley. Our bodies are obscene and we feed on the owls we catch in their lairs. We have voices like jackals and strike terror into the village children as they lie awake under the bedclothes. During the day

we scrabble about in the tombs, rummaging among the bones
and drinking putrid water out of skulls, and we ourselves have
the grey hue of skeletons.

You people flee death and at dusk you give the cemeteries a
wide berth; you have a horror of dead rats. Whereas we are in
love with these pitiable remains.

Don't come near us while you're alive; we hate you. But
we'll love you when you've become a cage of bones. Then
we'll watch over your destiny as perishable matter until you're
no longer recognizable and your ashes will cry out that God
has lost.

Here comes the black bull at the gallop. Our mother is
tied to its horns. 'Mother . . .' No, we have no mothers. Bull,
dash yourself against the rocks and kill her before our eyes.

What is there between us and you, Jesus . . .

You have come here disguised as a man just as we ourselves
are disguised as men. But we have long been familiar with each
other. Now we are face to face. We are playing for the eternal
lives of these human butterflies; for only you and we know what
eternity means; they don't. But the struggle is unequal. We
can only bait them with the fraud that all things come to an
end in a handful of dust. Whereas your words are pregnant
with hope, you have your tolling bells when they enter their
agony.

What is there between us and you that makes reconciliation
forever impossible? O Light, O Life, touch us and set us free
too, put out evil with your breath, call us back home . . .

But you've come only to cast us out and we are bound to
obey. It's horrible having no home, it's horrible floating about
in an inhospitable cosmos, being Evil unleashed in the air like
a lowering cloud. You knew, when you condemned us, what
a torture it was to wander about in space without the warmth
of a body.

At least let us go into those swine; they, like us, are creatures
made by the Father and under their bristles we'll still be in the
warmth of his kingdom.

The impure spirits left the obsessed people and went into the swine; and straightaway the whole herd of about two thousand plunged headlong into the lake and was drowned.

A unique enigma echoes through the gospel about this headlong plunge of the two thousand swine. There they go, flying over the cliff, a paradox of brute flesh preferring death to Satan, so harsh was Satan's company. Only man can tolerate it and live. Or is it that there's no sea big enough for our human flock to hurl itself into?

At this the Gadarenes were gripped by a great fear and implored Jesus to go away from the area.

After a crash and destruction like that, an exhausted fear lay on the people of Gadara.

'Lord, go away . . .' Reduced to terrorized shadows, the Gadarenes had nothing else to say. It was too tiring to try to understand. The only tangible thing was 2,000 pigs floating in the lake – their sole source of wealth gone. All they wanted was a village without conjurors or miracles. A village where you could sleep.

A FATHER, A MOTHER AND A
GRAIN OF SEED

'Ever since his childhood, the spirit has often thrown him into fire and water to destroy him: but if you can do anything, have pity on us and help us.' And Jesus said, 'If you can believe, everything is possible to those who believe.'

'Woman, you have great faith', Jesus exclaimed; 'let things be done as you want. Because of what you have said, go, the Devil has gone out of your daughter.'

These miracles on people possessed by the Devil took place within the miracle of belief. They were the most difficult miracles and the apostles couldn't perform them. *'Why couldn't we cast them out?' And Jesus answered: 'Because of your lack of faith. For if you had as much faith as a grain of mustard seed . . .'*

91

Jesus didn't touch possessed people with his hand. He stood still and at a distance; the froth oozing from their lips didn't splash his tunic. His voice was enough. *'Stop chattering and come out of this man . . .' 'I command you, come out of him and never go back . . .'* But for these miracles there was a price, and on this Christ was inflexible: faith.

A father, a mother: one sad story about each. Matthew sets down their appeals with what may seem excessive scrupulosity. *'Master, I implore you to have a look at my son, my only son; I've brought him to you, have pity on him. He's mad, possessed by a dumb demon, and he's suffering. When he's possessed and overcome by the spirit he shouts, foams, gnashes his teeth and becomes senseless. The demon only withdraws with difficulty, but first he rends him to pieces.'* And the other: *'. . . my daughter is being cruelly tormented by a devil.'*

But that wasn't enough. He answered the man with an outburst of contempt, and the woman with a dry, almost bored refusal. Where had the human Jesus gone? Once again he was the inscrutable prophet, the heartless stranger who once answered: 'Who is my mother? Who are my brothers?'

This time there was another long pause before the miracle was let loose. On one side were the people with their children who fell into fire and water – their arms hanging by their sides after they'd said their say; on the other there was him, alone, an intangible star. Even the disciples watched him in silence, in the middle of the group of disillusioned creatures who looked on him as an enemy because he'd said 'No'.

A great darkness spread around when he ceased to be Jesus of Nazareth and reverted to being no more than the Son of man – who didn't know our idiom of fathers and mothers and preferred a grain of faith in heaven to all the tears of earth.

But even this time he hadn't really said no. What he wanted was to turn two miracles of pity into two miracles of faith. And the blackmail levelled at the father of the possessed boy was all the more precious in that it overcame both the boy's epilepsy and the father's disbelief (*'If you can believe, everything is possible to those who believe'*). And the harsh words to the woman from Canaan were only a ruse to make her, too, pay the price the Father demands of us in order to give us back whatever we have lost: namely, the mustard seed.

THE WORD UNDER THE ROOF

'Lord, don't put yourself out . . . because I'm not worthy for you to come under my roof; and it was because of this that I dared to come to you myself; but just say the word and my servant will be cured.'

There's only one miracle really deserved in the whole book, and that's the centurion's one.

If it was granted to me to embrace just one of Jesus' followers, I would choose him – that pagan with a chest covered with war-wounds and a breastplate. He worshipped idols: Jupiter, Mercury, Venus . . . and war-gods too, Bellona and Mars. In Augustus's barracks in Rome they had taught him only one law, that of the strongest, and only one faith, trust in his own sword. And then one fine morning this soldier emerged from a dark and brutal existence into the very centre of faith and perfect charity.

The woman from Canaan (the other idolater whose faith elicited a miracle, and that, too, from a distance) acted for her daughter. The centurion at Capernaum acted for his servant. In Rome he'd been taught that servants could be bought, sold and beaten. By himself he'd learnt that a servant had a value and deserved not only affection but a humble petition to a subject of a conquered country (a thing considerably more difficult for a Roman world-master to understand, and requiring great courage).

In that place there was a centurion's servant who was ill, and the centurion was very fond of him.

The centurion's words and actions breathe a courtesy and liberality that might have belonged to the civilization of Horace and Seneca; but there was something besides that came from somewhere else, and this something was that he loved his servant. Among the wars of his hundred-strong squad and the gleam of victorious eagles, the captain hadn't lost his tender feelings for a human life; the man whose trade was blood and who had seen the death of cohorts was weeping at the pillow of his dying servant. The whole of the centurion's gospel lay in his servant – which was why he was already won over before he met Christ at the door. The servant was his plenary baptism: anyone who kept a poor man in his house and loved him really had no need to have Jesus under his roof.

Besides, he felt unworthy. Seven centuries of Roman pride in shreds at the feet of a barbarian, and a ragged one at that. *'Lord, don't put yourself out, because I'm not worthy . . .'* Yet even in these words there was a lurking hint of command. It's as though the officer's humility barred Jesus at the doorway of the house. *Don't put yourself out.* His voice was still rough and imperious, the voice of one who'd given orders to soldiers all his life and who, in all outward actions, still retained a rigid sense of rank, regulations and doing the right thing; and this reaction, based on manners, revealed the most delicate feelings in the centurion's heart. Now that he was face to face with the master he felt more than ever – though he had never heard him preach nor seen him work a miracle – that this man shouldn't enter his house: a word would be enough.

In the centurion's house Jesus' word met with old statues of idols, panoplies, trophies from Gallic lands, Numidia and far-distant Dacia. It took fearless wing, like a dove. Those ornaments were things that could do no more harm, they were dead. Whereas the servant was alive and already working about the house. The house of one of Christ's saints who would go on wearing breastplate and helmet.

BEATA DORMITIO

There's everything in the womb of the earthly valleys in which we pass our days. There's the house where we were born, the wood where the characters in fairy-tales got lost, the illustrated history-books about knights and multi-coloured caparisons; there's the sea and the ship which took us away from the only woman we could love; the country where we made our fortune and the one where we squandered it. There's October's lonely pathway, and the window-sill covered with early snow; there's night, day, the seasons, bed, the fireplace, war and dreams. There's a destiny made up of anguish and joy, the things we remember and those we've now forgotten. And last, and anything but least, there's death. This is the last word a human being learns because nothing with meaning or measure corresponds to it. Mothers don't say it in front of their children, eager though they are for words; we have to learn it for ourselves together with other words expressing the mysteries of life. Poets and musicians have sung it, painters have painted it, but the greater their efforts to describe it the more their metaphors repeat things which remain, uniquely, life. The horror of macabre frescoes, the booming of mournful funeral dirges, the lines of the darkest elegies, don't bring us a jot nearer to the enigma; they are just an orgy of images, fearful yet also still warm and quivering, and skeletons and funereal lilies are no less our familiars than the sun or a jolly dinner party, because they go to make up the only realm we know: the realm of things. Death frightens us because of its lack of things. Even in imagination we can't cross its colourless river. All we know is that it's always lying in wait for us, nestling here in our bodies and in the friend we adore. And what it will do to us is so horrible that we know of no hate which could measure up to it. All we have for opposing it is the despair of oblivion.

Christ alone has reconciled us with death. Only his saints have made it homely, caressed it in their caves like a tamed monster. *Beata dormitio* – joyful sleep: fragrant syllables which turn the nightmare inside out into a benign affair of nature, with an association of garlands, white pillows, and peaceful innocent dreams. Yes, since Christ, death retains a flavour of childhood, the day after the good news every name changed, the bier became a cradle, and Christ's family, with gay simplicity, was to call the death-day of his 'upright people' their *dies natalis*; the corpse was to be called a relic, and as it cast its

95

rays from the tranquil crypt it was to spread the scent of violets. At the touch of those bones the sick would be cured and there would be an outbreak of joyful miracles.

So we can die. In reality our death doesn't exist. It will coincide with the death of the world, it will snuff out our affections with our last gasp and awaken us in the Father's house. But there's another death, the only real one, the death we suffer with our eyes open, in the world that goes on rolling round us with the sun and unbelievable colours, and that's the death of those we love.

The purest of the saints, who for themselves invoked their passing as a festival, wept unabashed at the deathbeds of their friends. Christ, who with a smile raised two children from the dead, one at Nain, the other in Jairus's house, was to weep over the tomb of his beloved Lazarus.

So the three restored to life in the gospel were really more than three: their names weren't just Lazarus, the infant daughter of Jairus, or the fatherless child from Nain: they were also Martha and Mary, they were Jairus and his wife, they were the widow who accompanied her son to the cemetery, and they were Jesus, the friend, who in the end had pity on himself. Neither the lepers, nor the blind, nor the possessed caused such pain on the face of the earth as those dead people dressed in mourning, those living corpses bathed in tears who, by bitter fate, remained behind. Overwhelmed with compassion, Christ pronounced his miraculous command with the all-powerful spirit that could only come from God, but in the hoarse and frightened voice of someone who was merely a man.

TWO SUPERFLUOUS WORDS

When the Lord saw her, he had compassion on her and said: 'Don't cry.' And he went up and touched the bier. And when the bearers had stopped, he said: 'Young man, come and get up.'

This passage from Luke is very short but even so it contains two superfluous words. It says that the son was an only son and the mother a widow. This filled him with pity, and the detail suggests that our pity, too, should be more lively. As if anything could be left on earth for a mother accompanying her son to his burial; as if this could be a sorrow in any way measurable with other sorrows. But Luke was a man, and like us knew nothing of a mother's feelings: the angels don't know anything either and nor do the sons themselves. Mothers are a mystery of God.

We think we know women because we enter into them, because they drink in our words, they sleep in our beds and if we keep them awake telling them about our childhood they gaze at us in the darkness as though they were our very soul. But as soon as a woman has conceived no one knows her any more. She goes far away; she pretends to remember those days and nights, but we won't really see her again. Where do women go with that living morsel in their wombs? God alone knows. Luke doesn't, nor do the angels. And it's pointless to talk about them.

Anyway, all the words of this miracle are superfluous. All they do to us men is to make us feel emotional about a scene we'll never understand. All superfluous, except the words which conclude and sum up the miracle: '*Jesus gave him back to his mother.*'

He restored a dead man to life and to a fate that had been broken off. Christ gave this dead son back to his mother and his mother alone. The boy didn't rise from the dead for his companions or for the girls he'd courted in the early stages of the love game, or for the hill where he'd spent long afternoons setting nets to catch birds. The bearers might as well have pushed on and carried all that part of him to the graveyard. His friends could go and find him there for the short period in which people, other than mothers, mourn. There they could go and weep for him because for them the boy was dead, and when he worked his miracle Jesus had no intention of giving him back to them.

He gave him back to his mother. He, who had never touched a woman, was the only one to understand that mystery. He knew where mothers go, what happens to them when a son is born and when a son dies. He also knew this: the unnameable sorrow in that lament behind the bier, even though, when he'd stopped the procession, he only said what everyone else had said to her that day: 'Don't cry.'

DEATH IS A FLUTE

'Why so much noise and wailing?'

Flutes make a clear bright sound like the bleating of sea flocks, they scratch the air with ominous lines and curls, they people it with banners of icy brocade. On the crests of the world there appear throngs of strange animals, dolphins and lynxes which immediately turn their backs and disappear, screech-owls like witches cross the horizon, the whistle of their sharpest notes seeming to furrow the hour with blood. Someone throws javelins that stick in the ground to form improvised cages for fugitives. When the player strikes the flute's six holes with his fingers things change colour, the woman in bed and the hedgehog in his lair feel trapped – here come the monsters, where shall we hide?

'Your daughter's dead, so don't go on pestering the Master.'
Before the message from the synagogue reached him, the news was given by flutes to the child's father as he searched for Jesus. His heart was in turmoil as the fateful moments dripped away, and his ear was strained towards the house to hear the flute's first note. Streets, the clamour of early-morning markets, the bustle of shops; daily life was going on as usual, the life of the city, and within it *her* life; the noises of the city within which there was also the beating of *her* heart – because the flute was still silent.

It's a thin border-line between this side and the other, it's the note of a flute cutting through the morning air. First it wasn't there, then it was, because now it was already *afterwards*: the horrifying *afterwards* experienced in dreams, when
98

one leaps out of bed to wake up the beloved so as to hear her breathing, and says: 'Today when the sun's up we'll do this and that together . . .' But the flutes were still silent and we were still on this side of the border-line. And here was Jesus; the man ran and pushed his way through the crowd with clenched fists.

'Lord, I'd like . . .'

'Yes?'

And then the flute sounded.

'Lord, I've come to ask you, if you can, to make me die.'

Men take charge of death with their rites, they guard it like mastiffs from the very moment it's happened. And while those who loved the dead one are entering the always uncharted forests of suffering, the others – strangers acting in unison – entrust their impotent rancour at being survivors to various instruments and ceremonials. In this case they put flutes to their mouths and blew.

Christ passed through the orchestra of flutes which was venting man's agelong rebellion against death in the insidious alphabet of music – that blind rhapsody of dreaming slaves against the murderous master. Christ was smiling, a monster of gaiety amid the sobbing wake and the funereal clash of the instruments. In this passage of the book we find an impalpable wall of hostility between Jesus and other people.

'Get out of the way, for the girl isn't dead but asleep.' And they made fun of him.

What with the prophet's irony and the people's scathing reaction, it looked as if a nasty scene of lynching might be sparked off. The man who didn't believe in death and laughed at sorrow seemed hateful.

He went into the house and up to the girl's bedside, his smile remaining unchanged – but it wasn't a smile of irony. In the great dormitory of the dead, there in the house of his Father, he sought out a young girl who had gone to sleep too soon. And he took her hand.

'Get up, child.'

Outside in the portico the flutes were still breathlessly playing. With presumptuous enchantment they went on telling

99

a tale of caverns, of dawns with the whitest obelisks, of hoarse rivers, of butterflies with death's-heads. They went on describing death: that stupid thing which doesn't exist.

But by now they had become mere notes, a tune whistling in a six-holed tube, a noise of here-below like that of a hammer or a fountain.

The girl was eating.

THE FRIEND BEHIND THE STONE

Jesus loved Mary, her sister Martha, and Lazarus.

It was to that house, to that small gateway in strong old walls between the torrent of Cedron and the hill of Gethsemane, that he descended as often as he could when his travels brought him to Bethany. There they always kept a bed for him and a place for him at table, there a lamp was kept burning day and night against his fatigue and fear – visible from the dangerous and faithless confines of Phoenicia.

How did they meet? Why had he chosen them? Martha, Mary and Lazarus – sisters and brother – were orphans. In that house there was no father or mother to create an age-gap or disturb the trust that exists between contemporaries.

To the weary guest Mary's attention was a delight. She sat at his feet when he started talking, a straight parting dividing her beautiful hair. He also loved Martha as she bustled around with her housework (her sensible-girl's little bouts of ill-temper when she came in to get something and scolded her sister, who remained starry-eyed with the guest, when there was so much to get through); he loved the noises she made when, invisible in the kitchen, she was cooking supper over the fire. And it was pleasant for him, too, when on rare occasions the sisters left him alone and he could stretch out his tired feet, rest his eyes on the surrounding furniture, and look through the window at Jerusalem glowing in the sunset. From that peaceful hearth it looked like a lovely dream.

Lazarus was on his way home. Someone has said that Lazarus

was his disciple too; it's a mistake. True enough, the day was to come when, like so many others, Lazarus would face martyrdom for the sake of the good news, but that good news Christ had never announced to him. When he got back from the fields Lazarus put a friendly hand on his shoulder, sat down and began talking about the harvest, the olives, the lambs newly born in the stable or the pastures. Martha put a jug of honey wine between them, two mugs, bread and what there was in the larder for supper. Afterwards dice were thrown on the table.

Lazarus didn't call him master, rabbi or Lord. Just Jesus. And just Jesus felt at home between those walls, and his human side – hunger, sleep, gaiety – expanded in an ease which gave him fresh strength; he drank the sweetest wine on earth, friendship.

His divinity never passed through that door, the little square room wouldn't have contained it. It was as if he left it outside on the threshold – the crown was too dazzling: and it was as a human shadow that he entered the house at Bethany.

In that house he didn't talk in parables and didn't perform miracles. The brother and sisters knew how great he was, they knew about every single action he'd performed since the last time he'd eaten at their table. But they never asked him any questions when he pushed open the door without knocking and only said: 'Peace be with you, it's me.'

When Jesus saw her crying distractedly and saw the Jews who were with her weeping too, he trembled and was nervous. Then he asked: 'Where have you put him?' They answered: 'Lord, come and see.' Jesus wept, so that the Jews said: 'See how much he loved him.'

There's a long preamble to the miracle of the raising of Lazarus and this gives rise to speculation. Several days passed between the time that the news came that he was dying (*'Lord, the man you love is ill'*) and the time when Jesus set out for Bethany. He doesn't seem to have done anything memorable or particularly necessary in those three days of procrastination in Transjordania while Lazarus lay in his death-agony and Martha and Mary were desperately entreating him. His calm was puzzling: people didn't know whether to ascribe it to fear of the Jews who had promised to stone him when he got back, or to the apathy of a heart that in some inexplicable way had hardened. Both emotions seem unlikely. When questioned he answered in abstract, evasive or absurd terms. On one occasion he said: '*Lazarus is dead and I'm glad I wasn't there . . .*'

Three days is a long time. The sun turned slowly in the sky and a lot of water must have passed under the bridges of the Jordan, especially to someone who was watching it idly from the reeds and had a rendezvous with death. What was going on in Christ's mind as the river flowed under his eyes?

It may be that this miracle wasn't written in the Father's book. He hadn't been sent on earth for the sake of his friends. The sick he had cured and the dead he had raised were strangers, people he'd hardly ever seen, lepers with unrecognizable faces, unknown bodies already covered in their biers. Except for a couple of jars of wine and two boatloads of fish, he couldn't give much to his own people. He couldn't give himself anything at all; perhaps this is the best explanation for his delay on the Jordan.

'I'm a man too, Father, and Lazarus is more dear to me than anything else because he's my friend, the small sweetness in this bitter journey which was your will. I know that if I rush to Bethany you'll give power to my hands and he'll rise from the tomb, but I'd only be performing that miracle for myself, for the sake of the small number of days left to me – because death is too cold if there's no fire to sit by waiting for it. Write this other miracle in your book, but let me offer it to you, not to myself. Give me back the man I love as if he were a stranger, wipe out those pleasant evenings from my memory, make him the same as all those other people whose names I don't know, who aren't friends but only brothers and sisters.'

The Father answered yes, because he and the Father were one and the same.

So Lazarus would rise again. Just the obstacle of moving away the stone, and then Martha and Mary too would rise again to joy, once that rigid puppet became their brother again, and once the bandages round his arms were untied and he could clasp their heads, numbed with tears, to his breast.

So why did he weep? Lord, we were happy, Lazarus was already breathing inside his death-wrappings, what you said was true, he was only asleep . . .

But Jesus wept, and his face was masked by tears. One person was to emerge from his bonds, but behind the bars of death whole multitudes of eyes appeared. He was weeping for all the dead who wouldn't rise, for the stones he was unable to move away in the boundless graveyard of the world, for those who slept alone without flowers and for whom no one would be waiting if they came back. Over this river with no bridges which divided the living from the dead, the river which his parables and miracles hadn't been able to dry up.

'*Move away the stone.*'

LAZARUS: What stone? There's no stone between you and me. The thickness that divides us isn't this stone; it isn't the endless space of the galaxies nor the mad gallop of the millennia.

You're disturbing me. I don't know you; I don't know that crowd nor those two weeping women who are calling to me; I don't know this body that's grown stiff with these four days in the darkness of the vault. My name isn't Lazarus. I haven't any longings.

Where I am there's the Father. I haven't seen him, he's transparent like the sea and we're immersed in him like shells. But to meet him is the end of our struggles, our reconciliation has been dazzling. I didn't ask his forgiveness for my faults, and he didn't ask my forgiveness for life. It's a mystery you can't fathom, he loves us even within the harm we've done and we love him even for the punishment of living and we're grateful to him even for the days we spent on earth.

But if it's necessary, and as you want it, I'm back. If for you the senseless wailing of those women is more important than my freedom among the dead, then throw me back among the living. Yes, roll away the stone. There you are again, Martha and Mary. You don't know what you're like, but I've seen

103

you . . . I'll try to love you again, I'll stroke your hair and be
patient and reason with you, my good mad sisters, just as if
you were wise. Because where I was I've seen you as you really
are, I've touched your hands and heard your voices.

Come into the house, my good friend Jesus. I've come back
to open the door for you again. For your sake I've come down
once more into this foreign land where they'll nail you to a
cross. Come along in for these last few evenings. I can still
remember which jar has your favourite wine in it.

I'm ready. Never fear; I'll put on a good act. I'll laugh and
weep for joy. As soon as the stone is moved away, the streaming
sun, the masks called people, the flavour of the light and the
air will change me from a dead man who didn't want to come
back to life into a living man who doesn't want to die. Life will
take me into its arms again, the scent of cedar and sandalwood
will burst into my lungs with all its memories, the merry-go-
round of my blood will drag the old passions back into my
frozen veins and I'll feel hungry and thirsty. And I'll be afraid
of dying once more, because you, who are my friend, will
erase Lazarus's secret from him if you want him to walk
straight among these poor dead people.

I'm ready: remove the bandages.

THE GIFT TO THE THREE

*. . . he was transfigured in their presence. His face shone like the sun
and his clothes became as resplendent and white as snow . . .*

There was an hour in which our friend gave us an astonishing
present. It wasn't an object or even a favour; in earthly terms,
we could call it a confidence; but such a deep and total confidence that the revelation wasn't just one intimate part of
himself: it was the whole of himself that he gave us, even his
bodily aspect. In that hour our friend made himself startlingly
beautiful for us, his whole being became a harmony, he smiled
at us as he'd never smiled before, and his splendour in the
pleasure of our company, his wordless transparency, was
104

perhaps enough to give us the impulse to say: 'Stay like that, stay true and happy for me as you are now. Don't let's leave this room any more.'

'Master, it's good for us to stay here. If you want I'll make three tents here: one for you, one for Moses and one for Elijah.' It was Peter who said that. He was speaking on top of a mountain and in the name of his two companions who had also enjoyed the privilege: James and John. Jesus reserved the privilege of seeing him in that miracle of beauty for those three. He didn't choose them because they were the most deserving, but arbitrarily, with no calculations in his heart: not as apostles, but as friends. He had taken them up the mountain paths in silence.

Three men, not twelve, were to get sight of the Kingdom in advance and know what he was really like, for they weren't used to seeing him like that every day. He wanted to put aside his human appearance for a moment; to test whether, when he cast away his mask and was dressed like sun and snow, their friendship would hold fast or change into fear.

Their friendship held fast. To the eyes of the three, when they awoke from the sleep induced by their weary walk, Jesus shining like a fairy prince didn't seem a stranger or a character in a persisting dream. At last he was the Lord, in all his natural credibility. That Jew dressed in a poor tunic, always the same, discoloured by sun and rain, with his face harassed by fasting and fatigue, had been less credible – more disquieting and suspect – with his claim to be the Son of God. There was no fear, no repudiation. Only a deep peace. And they craved to stay in that company (Moses and Elijah had appeared beside the Master, talked with him, and even their majestic ghosts didn't disturb the intimacy of that crib). *'It's good for us to stay here . . .'*

It's good, and for us who are made for enchantments it's a temptation to linger here where we're happy and forget the trials and destiny of the others down in the valley who weren't chosen. Perhaps this was Peter's first heedless act of cowardice.

But their joy was short-lived, for soon the three apostles had *fallen to the ground*, their teeth chattering *in a great fright*. A cloud had enveloped them (and it wasn't one of those sudden clouds in changeable Alpine weather) and from the darkness a voice sounded: *'This is my Son . . .'* The Other, the Father, had entered the stage and then everything broke and we were frightened. We'd like Christ to have been an orphan, without that cord binding him to mystery and setting him too high in the heavens.

'Get up, don't be afraid.'

All four went back to the valley *at break of day*. As Peter descended the path he was sulky and longing for the three tents up there at the top, the sweet life of a few intimates, without anxiety, and with no more death. In front of him was Jesus, clothed in the usual tunic discoloured by sun and rain.

THE PARABLES

No one has ever spoken like this man.

WE DIDN'T DANCE

When many of the disciples reproached Jesus for his difficult sayings and hung back or abandoned him, the Master asked Peter: '*Do you want to go away too?*' '*Lord,*' the fisherman answered, '*to whom shall we go? Only you have the words of eternal life.*'

So that's why they remained: because he had the words. If he had merely worked miracles they wouldn't have stayed. Peter called them 'words of eternal life'. And words of eternal life didn't only mean words that promised eternity, but words that gave a meaning to life, which would otherwise be meaningless. They stayed, therefore, because he spoke to them. The fact is that for mankind the word is everything, it's the most precious bond of communion between the shipwrecked, because it's only words they can cling to to keep afloat and alive. Words are the saving shore.

They stayed so as to hear him talking, and he went on board an anchored ship or sat on blocks of granite or on the top of a hill: and he spoke to them in parables.

The disciples loved these parables and they were all impressed by them. On the one hand they loved them as fairy-tales, and were boys again in all those narrative colours and whirlpools. They were points of rest in their difficult days. But on the other they reproached him for their obscurity: '*Now you're speaking clearly and not using any figure of speech*', they said to him as though relieved. It was their comment on his talk at the last supper.

It's true. Very often his stories are obscure, illogical and paradoxical. Who will ever succeed in interpreting the story of the wasteful and swindling steward who, in the end, is praised for his shrewdness by the master he has deceived? How could he say: '*Make yourselves friends with your dishonest profits*', if they also had to despise the tinkling attractions of Mammon? How could they extract good from evil without sinning, or be innocent and cunning at one and the same time? On such occasions the disciples breathed heavily and distracted themselves with some small knife or piece of fishing equipment they had in their pockets, or they caught the eye of fresh listeners and made a gesture of apology so as to keep links of solidarity between common-sense companions. But soon they were all hooked by his voice again. They raised their heads and went back to following him, open-mouthed; they drank in his voice if not his arguments. And the sound of his voice made them dance with bewitchment and happiness even though they remained seated.

And that was enough. It's enough if you dance when Christ is telling a parable. Malediction and catastrophe is the lot of those who don't dance, and there are still many of them. Jesus compared them to the boys in the squares: '*To whom shall I ever compare the people of this generation? Who are they like? They're like children sitting in the square and shouting to each other: "We've played the flute and you haven't danced."*' We mustn't remain just sitting in the square – for his flute is playing for us.

FRIENDS AND ENEMIES

I've made my upward climb and I'm in the domain of parables. I'm a story-teller too so I wanted to go to that little city created by Jesus the story-teller. Perhaps this is the part of Christ's life that interests me most personally, for here we meet the ghosts of his thought, the plots and characters he invented, not to amuse us but so that we could save ourselves at least by making our choice.

Here, as in apologues, we can talk with everything, even with sheep, fishing-nets, darnel-threads or pearls. I'd like to ask questions, I'd like to listen and understand. I know it isn't easy. Jesus himself said that he spoke in parables so that people should *see and not see, hear and not hear*. But I also know that this wasn't a paradoxical and intentionally confusing play on words: all he meant was that staying in the darkness, and failing to understand the mystery of the kingdom he was talking about, was inevitable so long as those people – who listened raptly to him and forgot to eat – obstinately insisted on remaining as they were; so long as they weren't converted.

Here are the characters, still now and for ever warm from Christ's lips and destined to play an eternal part in this city; here they are with their passions and their bond as living creatures.

I see a sheep. The cheerful shepherd unloads it from his shoulders and puts it in the sheepfold with ninety-nine companions. Its eyes are dim, it's covered in mud and its wool is torn. The shepherd crouches down beside it, feels it over, fondly combs out its coat, then calls his neighbours: *'Come and enjoy yourselves with me,'* says he, *'because I've found my lost sheep.'*

They all make merry round that mangy animal, to all appearances the ugliest in the flock. There's a tiny festival within the four corners of that pen; a herdsman's toast. But higher up there's a big festival: for he said: *'There'll be more rejoicing in heaven for one repentant sinner than for ninety-nine upright people.'*

I wander round the fields on the edge of the village. It's nearly evening. There's a landlord surrounded by a group of day-labourers. He hands out a coin to each. The faces of those paid first are full of happy amazement. They'd been taken on to work in the vineyard at the end of the day and there in their palms lies a liberal and unexpected reward, as large as that of their fellows who'd worked since morning. They disperse happily towards their homes, throwing up and catching their coins like schoolboys.

I go into a church, and stop just inside because my attention has been caught by a down-at-heel man in the shadows. He's the publican, a tax-employee. He's muttering some prayers with bowed head and striking his breast, and I can just hear his words: '*O God have mercy on me, a sinner.*'

Now I'm in the middle of the village at the door of a big house. There's a beggar leaning on the fine sculpted and embossed portal; he's covered with sores and his name is Lazarus. From inside the house comes the shouting and clatter of a gay banquet, music and the appetizing smell of good food. Lazarus as usual is waiting, waiting for someone to come out and bring him some left-over morsel – salami skins or a bone with a bit of meat still on it. But only sleek well-fed dogs emerge, and these dogs aren't disgusted by his sores but give them a careless lick, and this gives Lazarus some relief.

This time it's wounds, and in an inn outside the village. The wounds were inflicted on a certain traveller who was robbed of his purse on the Jericho road, and the thieves left him half-dead on the roadside. Another man (a Samaritan) took him on his horse and put him to bed in this inn and poured oil and wine onto his wounds. Now the Samaritan is moving on and says to the host: '*Look after him and I'll pay all your extra expenses when I get back.*' Then he takes out two coins and gives them to the host.

Another road, in the dust of the country in summer: a road leading to another big house with a tower. An old man comes down from that tower where he's been scanning the horizon with long-sighted eyes, and runs along the road, only he's forgotten his stick in his haste and is in danger of falling. He's running because the person coming towards him, a young man, can't run for he's weak with hunger. The two moving points on the road get nearer, the distance separating them gets shorter and shorter. The old man throws his arms round the young man and kisses him, but he can't say anything because if he tried to speak his heart would break. The young man says: '*I've sinned against heaven and against you, I'm not worthy to be called your son . . .*' But by now the old man has got his breath back and he turns to his servants (to his son he can do nothing but call him by his name, repeat to him that homely word, because the boy might have forgotten it, mislaid it among the nettles and stray paths of the *distant land* he's come from): '*Hurry,*' says he, '*bring the finest clothes and dress him in them: put a ring on his finger and shoes on his feet; bring the fattened calf, kill it, and let him eat and have a banquet. Because this is my son who was dead and has come back to life; he was lost and has been found.*'

We're in another big house, in a huge banqueting-room. And there's an unexpected crowd of guests around the scented table and shining plate. The guests are cripples, hunchbacks, blind people and beggars of every description, all with an embarrassed expression on their faces tempered only by the sort of euphoria that goes with anticipating a delicious dinner. And in the midst of all that contentment the master of the house is raging because the banqueting-hall isn't crammed full. So he issues his orders: '*Go out into the streets and along the hedgerows and force people to come in to fill my house. Because none of those who had been invited shall taste my supper.*'

And what's the meaning of those cries outside at a crossroads? A servants' brawl. One man has seized another by the throat, is strangling him and bellowing in his ear: '*Pay what you owe me!*' The second man manages to get loose from the fanatic's grip and throws himself at his feet: '*Only be patient and I'll pay you everything.*' But the first man thrusts him away and makes so much commotion that the guards come along and the debtor is dragged off to prison.

Someone has come into the village and is talking to me. 'You've seen them. These are my people, the ones for whom I came and to whom I've spoken so often from the boat. Sinners and failures, incompetent and unwilling people to whom no one wants to give a day's job, mischievous sheep who've escaped from the fold, little men with patched-up souls who are as ashamed in church as dogs, wretches with sores and fleas only fit to whine at some gentleman's door, spoilt sons who

113

blackmail their fathers or drag through the world so as to become womanizers and swindlers, chronic debtors sucked in and then spewed out by prisons, cripples, the blind, the lame: all these mad people who are waiting for the Great Day. . . . For them I've paced a thousand roads and worked a thousand miracles. For them I invented parables. But it wasn't to set them on the straight path or warn them; for one day (suddenly raising them to the level of saints) I said for their sakes something that caused scandal: *"The publicans and the whores'*, I said, *"will come before you in the kingdom of heaven."* I invented most of my stories so as to take up arms against their enemies who are my enemies too, so as to defend these poor little people with whom they didn't want me to eat and drink, and to exalt them in their unappreciated greatness. Yes; those stories of mine which you remember as surrounded in an aura of gentleness were acts of defiance and malediction. Defiance and malediction towards the conventionally pious, the oppressors and the pharisees of every race. Take another look round my country. Look them in the face. It's against their sin that I have fought, and will fight to the end of time.'

I move off. I find myself once more at the crossways with the day-labourers who have been working in the vineyard. They're still muttering and looking contemptuously at the coin on their palms. *'Those last people only did an hour's work and you've treated them like us who have borne the weight and heat of the day . . .'* And I say to these men, 'But he'd made an agreement with you for the money. And after all the money is his. Your fellow-workers who came for the last hour are men like you, they have a family just as you have. Christ hasn't paid them only for their work but also for their suffering when they were turned down, he paid for the distress of a day when no one wanted them . . .' The vineyard workers turn their backs on me.

I go back into the church. I approach that straight-backed man near the altar. He is praying silently but I remember his words: *'I thank you, O God, because I'm not like other men, greedy and unjust and adulterous, and not like that publican either. I fast twice a week and pay a tenth of all I possess . . .'* And out he goes, his head high. I ought to stop him and tell him he'll go home with Christ's contempt on his forehead.

I step over Lazarus at the gate of the big house and easily find a place at the rich feaster's table, Dives, who's polite and hospitable to me because I'm well dressed. I notice he's drinking heavily and I'd like to tell him to moderate his gulps of wine and share it with Lazarus outside. For not much later my host's voice will be calling from the darkness: *'Father, take pity on me and send Lazarus to moisten the tip of his finger to refresh my tongue, for I'm agonizing in these flames . . .'* I see his five brothers beside him, eating heartily, and I'd like to have a frank talk with them about what's going to happen if they continue to ignore that heap of rags leaning against the door (*'I beg you, Father, to send him home to warn my five brothers of these things, so that they won't come to this place of torment too'*). But I decide it's not the faintest use talking either to him or his brothers. *'If they don't listen to Moses and the prophets they won't believe in a dead man raised to life'* – that's how Jesus ends this parable. They won't believe me either. Dives pours me a drink and looks at me out of his eye as watery as a seal's: 'Good health,' he says, 'good health.'

On the road from Jerusalem to Jericho, near the man coshed by the robbers, I'm waiting for the two travellers who I know won't stop. Here comes the priest, here comes the one who *sees that man and passes him by*, and shortly after along comes the Levite who *glances and moves on*. From where I'm standing I examine the two faces: those portentous faces on which (unlike the Samaritan's) there's no trace of pity. But it's no face I see: beneath the turban there's a kind of smooth colourless egg.

This other one, too, has a face like a big egg – the young man coming along another path on his way back to the big house with the tower. He slows down when he hears the noise of music and dancing coming from a window, but in his case the shell he has for a face suddenly flushes with rage. A servant has told him what's happening: '*Your brother's come back; and your father has killed a fattened calf because he's got him safely home again.*' This being so, the young man doesn't want to go in, and when his father comes to beg him to do so, he gesticulates and shakes his ovoid mask. '*Look,*' says he, '*I've been serving you for many years and have never disobeyed your orders, and you've not even given me a young goat to feast on with my friends. But when the son comes who's squandered his goods with prostitutes you've killed the fatted calf for him.*' '*My son,*' groans the old man, following him as he walks away, '*you're always with me and everything that's mine is yours . . . but . . .*' The eldest son isn't listening and is already a good way off.

Where's he going? He's going to join some other people who've also refused to attend a banquet ('*A man prepared a banquet and invited many guests. When all was ready he sent his servant to tell the guests: it's time to come . . .*'). Here we have yet more people without eyes or noses. '*I've bought a farm and I've got to go and see to it; do please excuse me . . .*'; '*I've bought six yokes of oxen and I'm going to try them out; do please excuse me . . .*'; '*I've just got married so I can't come . . .*' How could they possibly talk together and enjoy themselves if they haven't got faces? How could the farm man see his farm and the ox man his new oxen? And how could the young husband kiss his wife if he hasn't a mouth? And who will attend that good gentleman's banquet? Do you remember? Cripples, the blind, the lame. Their limbs are all over the place and they use crutches, but at least they've got faces and eyes, some have three eyes, five eyes, and can lend one to the blind; they've got mouths for laughing and eating and ears to hear the jokes and outbursts of their neighbour at table who's been drinking and never stops talking. Another who will come is that servant, still purple and speechless, who was half-strangled by his creditor, the creditor who said: '*Pay what you owe me*', and wanted his hundred pieces of silver at all costs though a few minutes before his master, moved by pity, had let him off his debt of ten thousand talents.

'What would you have me do?' Christ asks over my shoulder.

'There was nothing to do but weep, or else make war on such people, talk every day, never lose an opportunity to tell them how much they disgusted me and how much I was on the side of their victims – on the side of Lazarus, the man on the road from Jericho, the younger brother . . .'

I return from my stroll through the small city. I've met the hateful people, I know that they're the prisoners of their destiny and live in Christ's angry contempt. But I'd like at least to understand and help one or two of them – of these slow-witted, cowardly and stupid people of the parables. It's night now, and there's a lighted window and inside somebody is still up. I draw near. It's the rich man to whom his land has brought enormous profits. He's still awake because he's got a problem, and he confides to me: '*I don't know what to do – for I've no more storage space for my harvest.*' He has a think and finally says: '*I know what I'll do; I'll pull down my barns and put up bigger and better ones where I'll gather in all my produce and goods, and I'll say to my soul: "O soul, you've got enough goods in store for many years to come; you can rest now, and eat and drink and be merry".*' His face is large and self-satisfied. He casts a sympathetic laugh in my direction as though my presence has helped him to make the decision that has brought him peace. Off he goes to bed and puts out the light. I give him a shake and say: '*You're a fool; your soul will be asked back this night as ever is, and who'll get all the things you've stored away?*' But the man can't hear me. He's already asleep; or perhaps . . .

Darkness. Down below there's a twinkling of lights and a whispering of people still awake. Soon, at midnight, I know there'll be a cry of: '*Here comes the bridegroom, go out and meet him.*' I'd like to buy a jug of oil but the shops are shut. I hurry. Crouching against a trellis of jasmin are the five stupid sweethearts who have fallen asleep in the deep scents of the night, their lamps empty on their knees. The five prudent girls, on the other hand, are standing erect, their lamps throwing out a bright light, and they're whispering, '*Wake up*', and shaking the five sleeping ones, '*You never know the day or the hour . . .*'

So off these run to look for oil – someone will surely lend it to them. Yes, they get hold of some and here they are back again, knocking at the door where the bridegroom has entered with the five prudent ones: '*Lord, open up to us!*' But he answers from within: '*I don't know you.*' Too late.

I'm tired. On my way back to the inn I see someone crouching on his knees in a kitchen-garden and scrabbling in the earth. 'What are you doing, you wretched man? You're the servant with one talent. Why are you burying it? When your master went away he trusted you to trade with it, as your fellow-servants are doing, and they're multiplying their treasure.' But the man goes on digging. 'I'm afraid,' he said, 'I'm afraid. He only gave me this one coin and I can't take any risks with it. I'm hiding it. When he comes back I'll dig it up and say, "*Here it is, it's yours!*" ' 'If you do that', I tell him, 'he'll blame you and call you a knave and a fool; he'll take away your one talent and give it to the man who has ten.' 'But why?' 'Because he told you, "*to people who have something, more will be given and they'll have abundance; but to those who have nothing, nothing will be given and even the little they have will be taken from them*".' 'I don't understand.' So I try to explain: 'Your logic and my logic don't mean anything to him. He's a strange master, you know, *one who reaps where he hasn't sown and harvests where he hasn't scattered seed.* He doesn't like your lazy avarice. You'll find he prefers the cunning and enterprising agent who makes friends through the money he's stolen. He'll have you thrown out into the darkness where people weep and grind their teeth.' 'But I'm afraid,' repeats the crouching man, 'I'm hiding it. Then when he comes back I'll say: "This is yours." '

It's daylight again and dawn is glittering over the landscape. The sower is already in the fields, his apron laden. I see him throwing the seed with wide happy gestures. I see him scattering seed on the roadside where it is soon gobbled up by the birds; on the rocks where the sun will soon scorch it; and in brambles which will surely stifle it. But I can't warn him –

he has a carefree, confident air, as if inspired by some ironic faith. The sower is Christ. And he sows and sows; and part of the seed he has in his apron ends up by falling in the soft soil and produces corn: *here a hundred per cent, there sixty per cent, and there thirty per cent.*

But, Lord, where shall I lie when you pass by so that your seed isn't wasted? What must I do so as not to be roadside or rock or bramble? I am all and nothing, I'm a thing that doesn't know what it is or where it is, a piece of blind matter avid for your seed. You throw where you throw and I am where I am. I can't move away, I don't know how to change myself so that your seed won't be lost. So you pass by, and I have a terror of the birds, of the sun, of all the life around me being a tangle of brambles that will stifle what little of your goodness reaches me. I'm terrified of being no more than sterile and bitter darnel.

Then there's that enigmatic story about darnel; my own story and everyone's for that matter. The one about the field where *a man sowed good seed and at night, while everyone was sleeping, his enemy came along and sowed darnel all among his wheat and then made off.*

Every evening I lie down like that field under the stars and I'm that tangle of different grasses and have no means of knowing which are good and which are weeds. But if I tried to get rid of my weeds, my field would be absurdly bald with nothing more than an odd tuft here and there. Within this true and terrible thought of mine, the good stalks and the bad stalks get inextricably interwoven; or perhaps they're the same plant divided into two, and one tip is horrified by the sister tip and yet is in complicity with it. When I perform some action with generous innocence, straightaway some selfish calculation crops up – in the impulse to help, a vain self-satisfaction; in the consoling caress, a hint of lechery; in my evening prayer of thanksgiving, some base superstition.

And other people would already have extirpated all the good grass to the point of destroying me. My fellows, like the impatient servants of the parable, are asking for me to be

117

THE PARABLES

condemned. '*Why is it that there's darnel there? Do you want us to go and pull it out?*' All the others, except you. '*No,*' he answered, '*because if you pull out the darnel you might also find yourselves pulling out the corn. Let both grow together until the harvest.*'

'Let both grow together . . .' That is, you let me live, you let me be myself: because you see some good corn in me and I don't know where it is to be found. Because you're patient. And every year your voice sounds even for my fig-tree with no figs, a voice excusing my sterility to the master of the vineyard: '*Lord leave it alone this year too, until I've cleared it up and manured it; and if it bears fruit in future, all the better; if not . . .*'

If not? Perhaps you'll let the master of the vineyard cut me down. Or perhaps you'll say the same thing to him next year, and the year after that, like a forgetful vine-grower who pretends he's growing old.

But there's one parable I would have liked to have heard from his lips more than all the others. Because you told that one without the delight of any narrative embellishments, with a dismaying effect that only your mother would have grasped had she been among the listeners. The way you told it had prophetic impact; but perhaps in your heart (which was that of a man who clung like other men to the sweets of life) you also had the unconscious illusion that this story would save your life and somehow obviate your destiny on the cross; and that people who heard it and understood it would forgive you. '*A man planted a vineyard, let it out to cultivators and went off on a long journey. In due course he sent a servant to the cultivators so that they could give an account of the vineyard's produce; but the cultivators beat him and sent him away empty-handed. He sent another servant but they abused and beat that one too and sent him away empty-handed. Then he sent a third servant and they wounded him and flayed him alive. So the owner of the vineyard then said, "What shall I do? I'll send my son whom I love, and perhaps when they see him they'll show respect for him." But the moment the cultivators saw him they began plotting and said: "He's the heir so let's kill him and we'll have the inheritance." So they drove him out of the vineyards and killed him. Now what will the owner of the vineyard do to them?*'

118

What will your Father do to us? He sent the Son whom he loved. We saw him and heard him talking: this extreme parable of his we've brought down from the realm of fantasy and turned into reality. 'Let's kill him,' we said, 'and we'll have the inheritance.' I'm not thinking of the Jews who crucified him: I'm thinking of us and the way we daily drive him from the vineyard and put him to death.

And what did his Father do? He didn't exterminate us, as it says at the end of the parable; but, according to the parable's last words, *he gave his vineyard to others*. What others? Not us. Who knows who and who knows where? But not these hypocritical faces of ours, not this arid garden of masters and servants. Perhaps to others who don't know him, don't burn incense to him and don't even mention him, but are desperately beating drums in a primitive forest. To others in whose hands the vineyard becomes an immense and glorious thing: a kingdom. And they'll give the kingdom to the enthusiastic merchant: '*The kingdom of heaven is like a merchant who sets out looking for fine pearls; and when he's found a pearl worth a great deal he goes and sells what he has and buys it.*' They'll give it to the woman who can leaven her cakes: '*It's like the leaven a woman took and mixed with three bushels of flour so that the dough was all leavened.*' They'll give it to the man who put his trust in the mustard seed which he took and sowed in his garden. And the mustard seed *grew so high that it became a tree and the birds of heaven sheltered in its branches.*

We make our nest in those branches, we squeeze up and chatter in our thousands of millions beneath that green roof. Who remembers those old stories, or the man who once told them? But even if we no longer know where that root has thrust itself, we're on the tree of his parables: *What is God's kingdom like?* . . .

LIKE AN OVERTURNED CART

Until one day that voice of his filled a mountain with people.

The mountain was called Tabha, just a hump facing the lake of Tiberias. But on that day (an unexpectedly windy day) the mountain became high; it wasn't a mountain of soil and rocks any more but a mountain of men and women swelling it to a hundred times its size, a crowd rising to the sky like a swarming hive of bees. All the people of the world, living, dead and yet to be born, gathered there because of a precise question waiting to be answered. Taken one by one, they hadn't the foggiest idea of the nature of *the question*; if any single one had been called from his camping-place and told to 'ask what's on your mind', he wouldn't have been able to open his mouth. Supposing Isaac, Miriam or Levi were questioned singly they'd stammer that they had an ulcer or a tumour or shingles they wanted removed. This was why they'd climbed up the mountain; this was why, as on other occasions, *the whole multitude was trying to touch him*. But gathered all together as they were now, their need was a different one, and so was their curiosity. They themselves didn't know what question they had to put to Jesus. But he knew very well what it was and that day he was going to give them their answer. They wanted to know about happiness; whether it existed, what it was, and for whom, why they were always so haunted by it in their thoughts, and what they should do to achieve it.

Then Jesus sat down. Today he worked no miracles on their crooked legs and leprous sores, but he tried out a miracle on the destinies of the people in that enormous crowd. He began talking and taught happiness: *'Blessed . . .'*

The streams between the rocks, the clover fields polished by the wind, the clouds that came low and got tangled with the beech trees, seemed to be listening every bit as much as the camel driver, the widow, the boy with freckles.

Who was blessed? Was he already talking about happy people? Weren't there to be preambles to this discourse, philosophical introductions and distinctions, rationalistic caveats? Nothing of the kind. *'Blessed are the poor in spirit for theirs is the kingdom of heaven . . . Blessed are the meek for they'll possess the land . . .'*

The poor, he began with them. I think the 'poor in spirit' are people who don't believe in themselves, prisoners of incurable timidity, those who have no imagination by which to plan a better future and no personality with which to achieve it. They are the poorest; the only thing they are masters of is hope but of a disembodied hope that they can't link up with any fulfilment. They are the silent ones who live without touching anything, or even wanting to; only they often look upwards to the clouds and the blue sky because they know the sky's a thing you haven't to argue about with anyone. The sky is theirs.

Whereas the land is for the meek. They will possess it as soon as they put a foot on it, whether ploughing it for others or fighting over it for others (such as emperors) and dying on it; then decaying in its womb where they've been hastily buried.

'Blessed are those who weep for they'll be consoled . . . Blessed are the merciful for they'll get mercy . . .'

Weeping itself is a blessed state. For his poor, Christ sows consolation at the time of weeping, when sorrow burns at the top like a candle-flame and the soul overflows in drops. Then weeping, and weeping only, makes us merciful, makes us feel pity for ourselves and for others; and when *we are mercy itself*, then at last there's no frontier between God and ourselves, and our tears mingle with his.

'Blessed are the pure in heart for they'll see God . . . Blessed are the peaceful for they'll be called the children of God . . .'

Though our bodies are so easily contaminated with the things creatures offer us, at least our hearts must remain pure. If I shan't be able to embrace God because my hands aren't pure, at least let my heart be saved in generous innocence so that I may see his face from the furthest gleam of the infinite.

And if we want to be called children of God, then let's enrol ourselves in the ranks of the peaceful – in this hardest of all warfares which means anything but living in peace and giving up the struggle, but instead means fighting for the most threatened and trembling of mothers, peace. She who calls us Abel, who wants us all alive and disarmed, so as to wipe out the name of Cain from the stuff of the world.

'Blessed are those who suffer persecution for the sake of justice, for

theirs is the kingdom of heaven . . . Blessed are you when men come to hate you and reject your name as abominable and say all sorts of wicked things about you – for my sake . . .'

Suffer for justice's sake: even when justice seems the most unrenounceable good and injustice the most insupportable evil? Are people who do that blessed? How, when? Always, at once; today – not tomorrow. Because for them, as for those who are persecuted for Christ's sake, the Kingdom, heaven, is already around and within life. Their eternity will be marvellous, and they'll hardly notice the moment of dying, for the Father will give them the gift of making no clear-cut distinction between the blessed state of the angels and the blessed state of their days of suffering here below. Because Jesus that day on the mountain called them blessed and rejoiced with them.

That was a great day and something big and immediate had to be done for all those masses of people who were suffering and dreaming of happiness. The world had to be turned upside down like a haycart with its wheels in the air. And Christ overturned the world. Those who wept, those who were hungry, those who were poor were hauled up in triumph to become objects of envy; the meek and the peaceful were made the bosses of the earth – it was their booty, wrested from their enemies; and in the pure Kingdom which had been awaited for thousands and thousands of years, the persecuted made the oppressors tremble. Justice was done.

Justice was done in a world turned upside down. And from that mountain of saints, like a cascade of lava, there now foamed down the announcement of desolation for the others: *'But woe to you, you rich people, for you've already got your consolation . . . Woe to you, you who laugh now, for you'll be melancholy and weep . . . Woe to you when everyone praises you . . .'*

The rich, the well-fed, the pleasure boys, the vain – those whom Christ cursed from that mountain – weren't, roughly speaking, those who frittered their time away in ease and debauchery, in feasting and hand-clapping. Everyone has run after these things and has attained them at least momentarily. Jesus wasn't that naïve or puritanical. The damned, the people excluded then and for ever from that mountain, were those who in the fumes of such passions were to separate themselves off from the others, day in day out, to the point of making them suffer and driving them away. For there's only one sin, that of not loving; only one curse, selfishness; only one forbidden word, enemy. To that conclusion Jesus' sermon went on. On to the clover field, the camel driver, the beech tree and the widow there fell other words that day, so that everyone could attain the state of blessedness.

'If, when you are bringing your gift to the altar, you suddenly remember that your brother has a grievance against you, leave your gift there at the altar and go first to be reconciled with your brother . . .' 'You've heard that it was said, "an eye for an eye and a tooth for a tooth". But what I tell you is that you shouldn't resist evil. When someone hits your right cheek, offer him the left one. If someone wants to bring you to court to take away your cloak, give him your tunic too. And if anyone wants to force you to go a mile, go two with him. Give to anyone who asks you and don't turn your back on anyone who wants to borrow from you . . .' 'You know what was said, "You'll love your neighbour and hate your enemy", but what I say is: Love your enemies, bless the people who speak badly of you, do good to anyone who hates you, and pray for the people who persecute and tell lies about you. If you just love those who love you, what merit or reward will you get?'

Then all those men and women who had climbed the mountain to touch him and be cured of some illness began looking at each other. Even those who were furthest away could hear the voice of that man sitting there brought to them by the wind. *'Don't judge, and you won't be judged; don't condemn, and you won't be condemned; forgive people, and you'll be forgiven.'* And the words he said rebounded to those at the back of the crowd from those in the middle as they turned round; and people frowned with astonishment, thoughtfulness, or shock. *'But when you talk, let yes be yes and no no, because anything more than that comes from the evil spirit.' 'When you give gifts in charity see to it that your left hand doesn't know what your right hand is doing.' 'If your eye causes scandal, pluck it out and throw it away.'*

In that huge crowd some people smiled, others wept, some were frightened by what he said, while yet others went away. But everyone was thinking, *'No one has ever spoken like this man'.*

Here and there someone whispered to his neighbour and the neighbour nodded. Every single one of them felt happy and at the same time under a curse. Everyone would have preferred not to have climbed the mountain, and at the same time would like never to have to leave.

HUMAN ENCOUNTERS

My pleasure is to be with the sons of men.

HOW ON EARTH?

Among the Pharisees there was a man called Nicodemus who was one of the leading Jews. He went to Jesus in the night and said . . .

This is me. Among all the characters on the stage of the Gospels, I'm probably this one (even if I often see myself in the publican, the prostitute, the leper): Dr Nicodemus, the petulant intellectual, the one who 'went to Jesus in the night and said . . .'

I would have gone by night; and often. On those occasions when I can't manage to sleep because I'm horrified by the day I've just spent, and afraid of the one that's dawning; when my brain, and the academic knowledge handed to me by my father and mother who paid for my good education, weigh on my mind more than any sin – then I get up and go to him. I don't even need to get up. I lie there in the darkness, my eyes open, and pester him. It isn't praying; it's provoking him; and secretly I hope to tangle him up and topple him over into my own superstitious atheist's drama; and at the same time it's an appeal for the answer that will bring me peace, an entreaty that he'll get down to the blackboard, cover it with solid round figures, and *prove* to me there's a God, that he's the son of the Father, and that after a long and happy life I'll go to heaven. It's a demand that he should put the seal of metaphysical certainty on the tortuous pyramid of my culture.

It's night. No one sees us or hears us. So, with an open mind, and in a gentlemanly way, perhaps I may wring this privilege from him and have him explain a bit . . . If the right atmosphere can be achieved, the magic connivance favoured by the hour and the tête-à-tête conversation. Basically we are sort of colleagues: *docti sumus*.

Nicodemus wanted a private lesson; and that's just what I want. An encounter of two pairs of eyes. Not that crush among the hunchbacked fishermen and prostitutes in the Capernaum slums, or beside the lake, or in the desert where you spent three days without a meal surrounded by people with bleeding feet; nor that scramble up a tree like Zacchaeus so as to see and hear him; nor, worse, being mixed up with his followers when they killed him, with the risk of . . .

So Nicodemus went to see Jesus and Jesus received him. And I'm going too and he opens the door for me too and asks me to sit down. 'How on earth?' the Jewish doctor says to him, and 'How on earth?' say I too. '*The truth I'm telling you is that anyone who isn't born again by water and the Holy Ghost can't enter God's kingdom . . .*' '*Don't be amazed at me saying, "You've got to be born again". The wind blows wherever it likes, you hear its voice but you don't know where it's coming from or going to.*'

'How's that possible?' Nicodemus and I mumble. Now he's very polite about my scholastic position and says, '*You're a master in Israel, and you don't know that?*' Nicodemus and I, trying to swallow his irony, say 'Forget it . . . Tell us once and for all, how on earth . . . ?'

Big clocks, small clocks, watches chop up the hours of the night (apparently equal to those of the day and yet so different) with their tick, tock, tick, tock, within the house which, with its bricks and furniture, is suffering like us from the anguish of existing and not knowing why.

'*If you don't believe when I talk to you about things on earth, how can you believe when I talk to you of heavenly matters?*' says Christ from the old armchair in my study, crossing his arms. This time too, he's escaping me. And he's being the questioner. 'Leave aside those distinctions between earthly and heavenly things,' say I, 'and talk to me of myself who don't know what heaven and earth are, and basically couldn't care less. I'm just frightened, hugely and continuously frightened of dying.'

'Indeed.'

'What do you mean – indeed?'

'Indeed God so loved the world that he gave his only Son so that everyone who believed in him wouldn't die but would have eternal life. For God didn't send his Son into the world to condemn the world but to save the world by his work.'

I get up. It's just as before. I can't remember whose house it is, whether he's come to mine or I've gone to knock at his. It's all the same anyway. What's certain is that it was night when we talked; that, like Nicodemus, I tried to catch him out for the nth time; that I'm leaving the house where I paid my useless visit; and that I'm in the darkness of a country road. And in spite of everything I'm feeling better. I'm even happy; humiliated, but happy. That may be because dawn's coming up, and the darkness – at least the external darkness – is thinning. And I'm thinking of his parting words:

'The light came into the world and people preferred darkness to light because their works were wicked. The truth is that whoever does evil loathes the light and keeps away from it so that the things he's doing won't be condemned. But whoever does good goes to the light because the things he does are open and as if fulfilled by God.'

So perhaps I'm not entirely wicked. I love the dawn and I still find consolation, even after my heavy defeat and with the salty taste in my mouth of someone who hasn't slept a wink. I'm only Nicodemus.

WHAT MORE SHOULD I DO?

'Good master, what should I do to gain eternal life?'

Someone else approached him with a question. The rich young man. Nicodemus was a man of curiosity – an intellectual obsessed by the question 'How on earth?' – and so he was basically a poor devil plagued by his brain. But the rich young man was ambitious: *'I've always kept the commandments; what more should I do?'*

He was an ambitious man in the noblest sense. He wanted to be perfect. O the innocence of youth! All young people aim at being perfect. It isn't pride, it isn't just ambition for a career:

it's a youthful, boisterous ardour, a lack of experience of life. We, disillusioned by age, would have been irked by such arrogance; but *when Jesus heard these words he gave him a gentle look and loved him.*

He loved him: because a very young man who still retains such goals as honesty and obedience and is committed in his life to *goodness*, inspires affection. And, though necessary, it seemed almost cruel to have to answer: *'Why do you call me good? And why are you questioning me about what is good? No one is good except God.'* He loved him, because that creature kneeling before him said – and it was the truth – that he'd kept the command-ments. Fine, my boy. A pure sincere young man who obediently carries out his duties is a very moving mystery. We want to ruffle your curly head, send you away and promote you to the kingdom of heaven.

But that young man wasn't a saint yet: he was rich. And he didn't know that what cut him off from eternal life was precisely the thing he had in superabundance. *'My sons, how hard it is for anyone who puts his trust in riches to enter God's kingdom. It's easier for a camel to pass through the eye of a needle . . .'*

What do such riches consist in, Lord? Why do they make salvation almost impossible for us? That's easy, Christ answers. Even when wealth isn't greedy egoism it involves neglecting other people's needs because one hasn't experienced them. Whereas the Kingdom means knowing other people. How can a rich man enter a paradise which means *knowing*: knowing others?

'But in that case who can be saved?'

It was the apostles who asked that. And here the gospel begins to get complicated. Who, they asked, can be saved? As if to suggest: no one. As though all of us were rich in one way or another. And there's truth in that too. For all of us possess some sort of riches.

Perhaps to throw all our possessions into the sea, to annul with a shrug all that the land-register enumerates as belonging to us – perhaps that's the least difficult side of it. But what about our other treasure? Our loves, our habits, our needs, our skills, the longings we have developed, the sweet poisons of our thoughts, fragments of matter or of dreams familiar to us alone? My children, that woman, my friends?

We go on believing that these are legitimate possessions of the soul whereas they are really *things*, those 'many goods' of the young man Matthew tells us about. How can I live without those boxes of photographs, those old papers and cards and trifles, all the relics of my life? And how am I to face old age without that bench in the sun in the public gardens, by the lake where the swans are? And if it's like that, who can be saved?

With God everything is possible.

But when Peter said: '*As you see, we've given up everything and have followed you: so what will there be for us?*' we find that the gospel, with its shifting transvaluations, ceases to dismay. '*And anyone who's left his house, or his brothers, or his sisters, or his father, or his mother, or his wife, or his children, or his fields for love of the kingdom of God and for the gospel, will get back a hundred times as much straightaway, even now, in houses, brothers, sisters, mothers, children and fields . . .*'

Straightaway? Even now? Then everything is mine . . . If I leave everything and follow him, it's perfectly all right to possess things again from the start. So can I be rich and yet blessed? Rich and yet your follower? But who knows how, when, and at what price?

That moment, however, was a time of defeat; for the young man turned his back: *he was saddened and went mournfully away . . .* And Jesus watched him as he went away: *he followed him with a sorrowful eye, then looked round and said to his disciples: 'How hard it is for people with possessions to enter into God's kingdom!'*

THE COMEBACK

But Zacchaeus stood and said to the Lord: 'Look, Lord, I give half my possessions to the poor and if I've ever cheated anyone I give him back four times as much.' Jesus answered: 'Today salvation has come to this house . . .'

That day we really had the rich man's comeback. On that day riches were freed: there occurred a rare miracle, possible only to God, and the camel passed through the eye of a needle.

It still wasn't sanctity, Zacchaeus hadn't reached perfection: to reach that, as Jesus had said to the young man, you had to get rid of everything in the interests of the poor and follow him. All the same it would be terrible if that short little man hadn't come into the book: he was an enthusiast who turned up so as to mend in an unforeseen way a chain that seemed to have snapped, between the condemned world of possessions and the saved world of the gospel. An enthusiast without human respect who in the teeth of the prestige of his endless farms, his fine purple linen tunic, shinned up the sycamore tree like a monkey so as to catch a glimpse of the prophet (there's another characteristic of the cunning of the rich). For this reason Jesus shouted to him, perhaps with an amused smile: *'Be quick and come down, Zacchaeus, because I've got to stay in your house today.'*

Down came Zacchaeus, planning, from branch to branch, the delicious dishes he'd regale the Master and the other guests with, and calculating how much it would cost him to indemnify four times over the people he'd defrauded. But in his heart he'd already made up his mind, and in a moment he'd shout it aloud before everyone, and in an act of suicide both rare and worthy of a gentleman, declare himself a profiteer. And that confession, that signed statement, was the best piece of business in all his life. Even if the people around Christ continued to hate him and started murmuring: *'He's gone to the house of a sinner.'* But hardly had his feet touched the ground than Christ said: *'Today salvation has come to this house.'*

JESUS' HONEY

. . . and a woman called Martha welcomed him in her house. She had a sister called Mary who sat at the Lord's feet and stayed listening to what he said.

If I'm to turn Calvary upside down and side-step the garden of Gethsemane where he was to sweat blood and wrestle with his agony, perhaps I'd make use of that little house in Bethany, with its clayey soil, roses and sycamore trees. His drop of joy, his earthly *possession*.

A house, for the man who's never had a stone to rest his head on. The noise of pots and pans, of bread-bins being opened and closed, of water on the boil; and happy, lazy cats in warm corners. For company, two women. One always busy, queening it over things and yet being their handmaid at the same time, with the cheerful yet slightly aggressive attitude of housewives who are always behindhand; the other sitting at his feet and listening, accepting the tiny cowardice of becoming a child again, of surrendering to the lazy ecstasy of story-time.

Neither Martha nor Mary was in love with Jesus, although he came so often to their house and although he was Lazarus's friend (and falling in love with your brother's friend is a tender and inevitable pastime when you're young). And yet it was as if they were in love with him – if it be true that admiration, devotion, affection, gratitude and every heart-beat, in anyone born a woman, are none other than chaste metaphors of love: that continuous and bewitched self-offering.

In those hours, those afternoons when Lazarus was out working, Jesus enjoyed the essence of womanhood in those two creatures; the honey of life. Dreamy Mary was the pale nectar of the garden, agitated Martha a bitter honey from the Alps.

Christ's honey: woman. Transcending the senses. The Samaritan woman at the well, the forgiven adulteress, the Magdalen of the perfumes, the mothers to whom he granted miracles for their sons, all of them; and first and foremost Mary of Nazareth. They were his secret holiday, a sort of good news within the good news, the gospel in undertones without anger or nails: it was he who discovered woman, thousands of years after she'd been created, and by so doing inaugurated the soul of the modern world.

'*Lord, don't you care when my sister leaves me to do the housework alone? Tell her to come and help me.*' This *intimiste* picture from the palette of Luke, painter and doctor, ends up in an affectionate badinage: '*Martha, Martha . . . you get bothered by too many things . . . Mary has chosen the better part.*'

To be sure Mary chose the better part: Christ's feet, that edge of matting on the stone floor where all the world – springtimes, waters, loves, celestial gardens – was gathered together at the sound of his voice. But Martha, the busy one, wasn't all that different, she wasn't outside the circle, she was a woman like Mary. She came in and out, keeping the kitchen door open; and when her hands were in the flour she listened with one ear, and loved.

ANOTHER THIRST

'*Lord,*' exclaimed the woman, '*give me that water and then I won't be thirsty ever again and I won't come back to draw from the well.*'

What thirst? What water? At the wellside encounter with the Samaritan woman the conversation opened and remained within the terms of a water-thirst enigma. Water, with its natural and metaphysical charge, was mediator on that day between two worlds which had been inimical since ancient times: male and female, spirit and flesh. It was with the theme of water that Christ avoided the woman's sensuality – with that pure abstract thing so loaded with symbols.

Yet sublimated though it was in the chaste sorcery of water, the start of the conversation was vigorous and expressive: '*Give me a drink.*' The Samaritan woman was used to being asked for a drink and in ways less modest – she herself being the drink. Many a man had quenched his thirst with her! Christ reminded her of this: *'You've had five husbands and the one you've got now isn't your husband.'* But that was the sum of his 'sermon' on her dissipated life: a bitter and ironical enumeration. He went no further. Jesus' peculiarities were always unpredictable and this time he chose to embark on a theological discourse: *'. . . anyone who drinks the water I'll give will never thirst again; indeed the water I'll give will become a fountain that will gush for all eternity'*; *'. . . the time has come when you won't worship the Father either on this mountain or in Jerusalem'*; *'. . . the time has come – and this is it – when the true worshippers will worship the Father in spirit and in truth; because that's the way the Father wants his worshippers to be. God is spirit and those who worship him should worship him in spirit and in truth'.*

And the woman, *that* woman, provoked by an idiom she was so unused to, gave him the most delightful answer: *'I know that the Messiah, that is the Christ, is about to come; and when he comes he'll tell us everything.'*

There she is, a theologian; but her theology, beyond reproach as it is, was typically concrete and womanly: 'A man will come . . .' We're just like her and can't understand a thing about God as spirit. All we can do is be like her and accept the knowledge that someone will come who will 'tell us everything'. And now that the woman had no more reserves – the pitfalls being overcome and everything being in a state of wonder and in an aura of innocence – it was appropriate that Jesus should make himself known to her, should give her the dazzling privilege of his self-revelation: *'I, who am talking to you, am that man.'*

Now the Samaritan woman knew the gift of God (*'If you knew the gift of God and who it is who's saying to you, "Give me a drink" . . .'*). Now and for ever her thirst was over because the water offered by Christ was living water and quenched all fires – even the daily fire in our bodies which seems so gay and makes us all brothers and sisters of that provocative water-carrying girl who, a little while ago, brashly challenged Jesus at the sixth hour by Jacob's well.

So also for us that's put paid to the disquieting thought that

Christ won't talk to us because we're Samaritans, that is children of the flesh. Today there shines before us the hope that he wants to reveal himself first and foremost to us, precisely to us. When the disciples go off to do the shopping and we get the chance to be tête-à-tête with him beside a well.

FLESH AND STONES

'Woman, where are your accusers? Has no one condemned you?' And she said: 'No one, Lord.' 'I don't condemn you either. Go now, and don't do it again.'

The step from sexual pleasure to death can be extremely short. For a Hebrew woman it was enough to be caught in the act of adultery. The trial was very speedy or didn't take place at all. And an incautious woman could be torn from the darkness of her lover's caresses into the glaring and shameless light of a public square. She would be dragged along to the scandal of the populace with scarcely time to shrink into herself as if to annihilate herself to avoid being the target of cruel eyes and stones.

That there could be extenuating circumstances, such as that the woman was unfulfilled, persecuted or misunderstood, never seems to have entered the minds of Hebrew judges. For that fault there was neither trial, reflection, nor 'factual' reconstruction. 'Moses commanded that such people should be stoned to death,' said the scribes and Pharisees to Jesus, 'and we've no intention of disobeying Moses.' And loiterers in Jerusalem – good womanizers and even, perhaps, voyeurs – thought but didn't say: 'Whatever happens, we don't want to miss such excellent entertainment on this sunny afternoon', and they licked their lips.

Our moralistic stone is no more than revenge for not being the lover ourselves.

Jesus knew all this, but so far he hadn't opened his mouth. He'd been asked for his opinion impatiently and repeatedly. He'd bent down and written on the ground with his finger.

Not only the men clutching their stones, but even the woman became impatient. Not that she nursed any false hopes – she just wanted the business to be over and done with. But Jesus remained deaf and distracted and continued writing on the ground. Not words, perhaps, just arabesques. Some exegetes have supposed that Jesus was noting on the soil the sins of the people standing around, the people most pressing in their desire for a condemnation. I don't think so. But we may be permitted to think that each of those men trembled inside when he saw traced on the ground among those hieroglyphs some unexpected name or place or date he recalled only too well.

Then at last Jesus made up his mind. 'Very well,' he said, 'start. . .' Stoning to death? Of course. But in a competition of this kind, over a matter of honour and justice, it was only right that there should be an order of precedence, a sort of rough etiquette: *'Whichever of you is without sin should be the first to throw a stone at her.'*

'What a paradox, Lord! Do you imagine that an innocent person, a man of honour, would throw stones at one of God's creatures? You do really understand, don't you, why I'm putting down my stone and making off? It's because I'm blameless and have no ill-feelings and don't want to get mixed up in a crime.'

So one by one the gentlemen went off. Not because they were weighed down by sins, not because they, too, were unclean and adulterous! But because 'sinless' people didn't commit cruelties like that. They put down their stones quickly and carefully so as not to make a thump, and they moved off with grim resentment against the spoilsport.

When the two of them were left alone Jesus tasted a moment of glory. The perfection of his heavenly diplomacy which had warded off a murder almost amused him. Those Pharisees and publicans who had sloped off behind the columns of the temple were a farce. Jesus also savoured a secret triumph as a man, and this made him happy. He was happy at being stronger than Moses ('I don't condemn you either'); at being more seductive in his smile at her ('Go now, and don't do it again') than the lovers still waiting for her, and more seductive, too, in the insidious sweetness of that new way of living he had presented to her.

TWO ALABASTER VASES

'If that man were a prophet, he'd know for certain who the woman is who touched him . . .'

Who touched him this time? She was a sinful woman who lived by selling her body. In her world scents were aphrodisiacs, they were part of her professional weaponry; and long hair too was an aphrodisiac, that hair which she used to dry Jesus' feet after bathing them with tears and ointment the day he dined with Simon the Pharisee. Very expensive ointment. That alabaster vase must have cost her the profits of many nights of mercenary caresses. And now all the contents were poured on his feet.

The girl from Magdala was one of those – like the adulteress and the Samaritan woman at the well. Simon's guests, though they may all have slept with her at one time or another, now avoided her and looked the other way as she stepped across the room to reach the Master. But Jesus felt neither distaste nor embarrassment at her touch. He felt the scented liquid flowing over him from the broken vase. He breathed in the sweet perfume. Then he felt her hands on his ankles as they spread the liquid and massaged it into the pores, and he watched her bowed head when her hair, with its soft warmth, dried his feet again. He looked at that young body which on this very day, at this very moment, had closed itself to its pleasures. He felt the tears pouring from her beautiful eyes and knew that in the very act of her repentance many of those tears were mourning for the pleasures she would know no more, were her farewell to youth: they were tears all confused in a whirlpool of love. Henceforward Magdalen's love was to be of a different kind – without music or brazen laughter or sexual rapture. But it would still remain on an equal scale. It would be a love that renounced men's embraces once and for all – until that day, not so far ahead now, when at dawn in a garden near an open tomb she would try to embrace a dead man who would stop her and say, 'don't touch me'. But today there was still delay in that scent and those tears: delay in the touching and kissing of that man's feet – her last act as a woman. *'It's for this,'* Christ murmured to Simon, *'it's for this, I tell you, that her sins are forgiven, because she's loved so much.'*

By this time the hair of both Jesus and Magdalen had the same scent – the sharp, Eastern and rather equivocal scent of nard. And we've no reason to suppose that that scent won't be the first sensation to invest our nostrils in the Elysian fields. For Christ said clearly: *'Whores will be ahead of you in the kingdom of heaven.'*

'I'm telling you the truth: wherever this gospel is preached, what she did will be told in her praise throughout the world.'

Jesus was also gently moved before that other bent head, the one in the house of Simon the leper. The parting dividing that young head of hair, and the shape of the brow, were already familiar to him. In Lazarus's house she had often been close to him like this, at the level of his knees, so often urging him to talk; and now for the last time. It was the lot of Mary of Bethany, this mute and crouching woman, that we shouldn't know anything about her height or her voice. And with his great praise Jesus rewarded on that day not only her scent but her long patience as a listener.

There may have been an odd wink here and there, and some nudging among the guests, as always happens when a man and a young woman get close together and shut themselves off in a circle of intimacy. But if there was anything in this, Christ had no desire to acknowledge the ripple of malice. He knew this was an operation dealing not with life and the senses, but with death. And nothing is more chaste than death and the way we treat a corpse.

So he said to the others there: *'By pouring this ointment over me, which she had kept for my burial, she has anointed my body in advance.'* He knew that for Mary of Bethany his passion – which lay three days ahead – had already happened, that very moment and in

137

that cheerful dining-room, and it was as though he were already hanging from the cross and her hair were attempting to dry not only the spikenard but also his blood. Like austere old Simeon, and Mary his mother, this small woman was a prophetess of his passion and the first witness of Christ crucified.

But someone was jealous of this funereal idyll and scandalized by so much waste. *'Why squander the ointment?'* some of the disciples muttered. *'Why not sell the ointment for three hundred pence and give it to the poor?'* went on with shrewd orthodoxy the disciple who was to betray him for money. As Matthew puts it: *They fumed against her.*

When Jesus noticed this he said: *'Why are you molesting this girl? Leave her in peace. She's done me a good turn. For you'll always have poor people among you and you'll be able to do good when you want to; but you won't always have me.'*

Another of the Master's lessons. To the charity accountants. To the gospel-swindlers attempting to usurp its doctrine and twist it against the canons of love. But I can hear a cry of applause for the phrase. I can see all the poor of the earth crowding round the scene in Simon the leper's dining-room and throwing their meagre money on the floor so as to pay for the three hundred pennyworth of scent. 'We'll always be here. But this man who is going to be betrayed and nailed up naked on the hill is really the poorest of all and you'll only have him with you for a very short while.'

Mary hadn't even heard the snarl of voices raised against her. She calmly anointed her Jesus with the specially feminine diligence that women, whether mothers or prostitutes, lavish on that jewel which is the body. That was her way of making him incorruptible for the resurrection. And she believed in resurrection more than anyone for only a few days earlier she had seen her brother coming out of his tomb alive. And that was why, if she alone was suffering in that throng of cheerful people, she was also the most inwardly serene: for she knew well that her ointment wouldn't be wasted.

THE BIG THRONG

'Let the children come close to me . . .'

. . . you stay around, little ones, and don't be frightened by the men who call themselves my friends yet have shouted at you and tried to chase you away. Be sorry for them. Tell them that it's only because you exist that I can endure the presence of the grown-ups: it's only because of the time you spend with me, as you're doing now, with your running noses and big greasy heads, and your shouting and shoving and treading on my toes, that I can overcome my disgust for their honeyed tones and their limbs smeared with ointments. It would be terrible for grown-up men if I couldn't see behind their beards the little freckled faces, the mouthful of strong teeth and the cheeky grimaces you make when you dance around me. If I say 'amen' when they draw their last breath, it'll be because I've forgotten all the things they've done since they were your age and played with tops and kites. Soon I'll be taking into glory a highway robber, but only because his groans from the cross beside mine will sound like the unbearable crying of a beaten child. But you won't feel frightened when you meet him after death in the Kingdom, or even when you meet Judas, Barabbas, Caiaphas and Herod. You won't be able to recognize them. I'll gather them to me at the point at which you are now, just like any other child who's all fear and boisterousness, fits of temper, sadness, kisses – but not sin.

It was to protect you that I pronounced the worst of all my threats. One day I said that anyone causing scandal to any of you would do better to drown with a stone round his neck so that no one could fish out his body. But I know that you're not all innocence. I love you all the more because of that tiny flicker of evil that's already disturbing your blood, because I see the dragon's teeth already in your innocent flesh that didn't ask to be born. That's why I'd like to keep you here, as now, in this big happy throng. If it weren't for the thought of your

139

mothers, my strongest temptation would be to cover you all up with my red tunic and fly with you straight to the bosom of our Father. Not to stop you being corrupted (I know that when you cease to be lambs you'll stray into the ravines like all my sheep and may become adulterers and murderers) – no, not because of that; since my blood will wash away all the sins of the world; but so that you may be spared all the sorrow awaiting each and every one of you, the thing I can read on your curly foreheads and on your scratchy hands; so as to save your bodies, as pink as fishes, from old age which consists in waiting for death.

Soon we'll be parted. The disciples will drag you roughly away from me. Go home. But remember that for me only you are men and women. To you I'll give my mother as a present from the cross.

Remember that we'll see each other again on that day, and we'll see each other as we do today even if death comes to you when you're bent with age. At the very moment when your soul detaches itself from your exhausted body, be quick and grow small like this, so as to be back again at this precise instant in this tangle of toys and bumps on the head, so as to wipe out puberty from your bellies, so as to recover your unbroken voices and deafen me with your shouts in the Kingdom. Otherwise we won't meet again, forgiveness would be impossible even to my Father's mercy; and there'd be darkness.

ALL WITH HIM

. . . one of his disciples said to him: 'Lord, teach us to pray.' . . . So he said to them: 'When you pray, say: "Our Father . . ." '

The hardest lesson. Who had ever managed to pray? What is prayer? The master of prayer, he who had the habit of fleeing to the mountains for whole days on end to talk with the Father, had already told us about this mysterious thing which is impossible to mankind – alike fascinating and repulsive. Some preliminary rules ('*When you pray go to your room, close the door and secretly raise your petition to your Father, and the Father, who can see into secrets, will listen to you . . .*'; '*When you pray don't use a whole lot of words as the pagans do who believe they are heard because of their avalanche of words . . .*'); impassioned syllogisms to win us from our scepticism ('*If any of you are fathers, would you give your son a stone when he asks for bread? Or if he asks for fish, would you give him a snake, or instead of an egg put a scorpion in his hand? . . .*'); and finally: '*Your Father knows your needs before you've asked.*'

But praying was still an empty act of acrobatics. The door always remained just open enough for God to go out and men to come in; and moreover too often – perhaps almost always – after asking for an egg with a multiplication of words and a deluge of tears, as the pagans do, we found the scorpion in our hands – grace denied. Finally, the very awareness that the Father – the extremely intelligent scrutinizer of our innermost being – already knows what we need, froze our prayer on our lips, almost with ironical shame about a game for which we're now too big.

Thus, even though David, Isaiah and Jeremiah stammered their stupendous psalms in their attempt to speak with God, prayer remained for man a sealed-off island, a disconcerting act of powerlessness; confusion of words; often enough the spiral of a nightmare. In truth no one ever prayed before those sixty or so words were uttered: '*Our Father who art in heaven . . .*'

When, why and where were those words born? I like to think with Luke that they came into being when Jesus had just emerged from the house in Bethany and his disciples, in a state of metaphysical confusion and disarray, accosted him with: '*Teach us how to pray . . .*' On the other hand, this was perhaps the Master's happiest day. He'd been in Lazarus's house, in Martha's and Mary's kitchen; and had just tasted at his friend's table the 'daily bread' he was about to exalt in his prayer; and in its fragrance – symbol of the sum of private joys it is permissible to ask of God – he had found the benevolence, the inspiration, the undramatized peace with which the Great Prayer is imbued. '*When you pray, say . . .*'

And we *say* – and have done so for two thousand years. And the prayer remains God's highest thing, yet fits our lips like the most natural act of breathing; it's as easy and earthly as a soldier's coming-home song, it's as lofty as a tower and as familiar as a nursery rhyme.

To bring the Father down from his beautiful yet ever remote heaven we only need that word 'our' which is more than an adjective – it's an imperious and victorious shout, a surprise action, the capture by a majority of a king who becomes a hostage.

Heaven: here lies a love whose face it is no longer necessary to decipher once we're in possession of a name – *father*. And in *hallowing* that name, in making his kingdom *come* among us, in letting his will *be done* beneath our roof, that face unveils itself to us, emerges from its obsessive abstraction, and there's no more need to raise our eyes to heaven because clouds and meadows – *sicut in coelo et in terra* – form one and the same circle for us who are freed from evil.

Libera nos a malo. The evil that goes away, the bread that glows on the table, the temptations that give us a truce: the few gigantic things needful to man. They're requests, petitions, but as we say them they seem to be already gifts obtained and matters settled. In these seven phrases there's only one bond on man's side, the coin with which all the rest is bought: to forgive those who trespass against us, as he forgives us our trespasses; *to forgive*. Who said that God was mercy? He's rather the good tyrant who condemns us to mercy, who'll only learn it from us when he sees us vowed to mercy. Tyrant and servant at the same time if he awaits from us this command: '*Forgive us* our trespasses *as we* forgive them.' God's conduct is entirely in our hands.

The rest – praise, petition – Jesus tells us is beautiful but superfluous ('. . . *the Father knows your needs*').

Let's cancel our credits: we'll have prayed already. Christ himself prays the unique and living prayer as on that day. He prays it even if we unwittingly fall asleep. While we're sleeping bushels of joyful wheat will fall into our lap. '*A good measure, pressed and shaken and overflowing, will be poured into your laps because it will be measured out to you with the same measure with which you yourselves measure.'*

Since that morning when the Son spoke for me to the Father it's no longer impossible for me to pray. It's no longer a matter of setting going a mechanism of piety and fear. It's stretching myself out in Christ's company. I despair of my life and he tells me ancient stories about myself, he pours into my soul wonderful hours that I'd forgotten. I'm in anguish for someone who's died and he takes on the face of that dead person and tells me his secrets. I look at him: I know well that he's an unattainable model; but he traces that perfection before me without crushing me. He never converts me, but now and again he sets me straight. Even when he says, 'this isn't a sin, my friend: it's a mistaken way of reaching a better understanding of each other'.

In repeating the sixty or so words we meet everyone with him, according to his will. For Zacchaeus, the Samaritan woman, the rich young man, Mary and Martha aren't enough for him. We meet under the pergola of Bethany and under the open skies of the Father.

THE CITY

And then Cain built a city.

THE EXILE

When Jesus was near the city he looked at it and wept over it . . .

From a hill above. Perhaps a natural seat of rock or root. He saw it from up there as it lay nestling in a shell, its houses and domes and blobs of trees taking on that air of innocent humility which even the most dreadful and wicked cities assume from afar.

Had you wandered through the streets and along the alleyways the city would have seemed one great sore of arrogance. But from above it looked something else, no longer the sum of its stones, or of the misdeeds, rancour and despair of its inhabitants. The city seemed good and amazed as if behind a mirage, within a spell that was soon to dissolve it: it seemed suspended at its last minute between a cry of clemency and a huge envy that would soon fall on it and wipe it out. Anyone contemplating the city from a viewpoint on a hill, as did the Master, would be tempted to stretch out his hand in an impotent caress. But precisely because it felt impregnable, as safe as the stage of a theatre open only to the eyes that look on it, the city had from afar a shrewd recognition of its errors. It washed away the ugly spots of its murders, it camouflaged the corners where huddled its brothels, and when darkness fell its lighted windows vied with each other in telling a story of civilized friendship, as if in every house were gathered round the table a happy family giving thanks to God.

And precisely for this reason the city, Jerusalem, which lay only a bee's flight away, was sad and caused pain: because of that lie it was telling. In that outspread map of houses there wasn't a single roof that Jesus could recognize (as we try to do when we climb a church tower). With his eyes he sought the places where for three years he had played out his hard profession as God, the crossways where he had straightened the paralysed and the crooked, the little side-streets where he had given sight to the blind. Over there lay the pool of Bethesda with its sick people waiting; over there lay the temple from which he had driven with whips the blasphemers who were buying and selling, where the bent woman had been made straight and where the man had regained the use of his shrivelled hand. Unpleasant memories. For one friend sent home cured, ten or a hundred enemies had risen against him, had swollen day by day the great revenge. And there it was, only a few dawns away, the revenge that the city would wreak on the Son of man: that barren hill to the east, the mount of Calvary.

In scanning the hills with his eyes, Jesus foresaw Titus's legions gleaming on the plain, the army that was to be the revenge on the revenge: ... *there will come a time when your enemies will entrench themselves around you and besiege you and attack you from all sides, and they will destroy you and your sons and not leave a stone on a stone.* But nothing made him more disconsolate than this prophecy of carnage and punishment.

Yes, the city was wicked: every city is heir to that first city which rose from the earth in blood and remorse (*then Cain ... built a city which he called Enoch*). That was why there had been no room for him within those walls, and that was why he gazed at them on that day with the burning humiliation of an exile, with the shame of an outlaw. Within that swarm of stones down there, the lowest snake was queen in the crack of its well, a favoured daughter of the city like Caiaphas the High Priest, like Simon the leper; and a sister to the tax-collectors and scribes in the warmth of a common connivance, already waiting to shout from her little triangular head her own: 'Crucify him.'

Yet with its medley of lights and the idyllic colouring of the country, the woods, the sky, the city persisted in being pleasing.

And then, suddenly, in order that that pile of houses and gardens shouldn't tempt him again to love, a certain person who had already tried to seduce him in the desert whispered a final temptation in his ear: 'Curse this imposture of stones and steeples, spit on it, go on, spit! Then make your escape.'

But this time Christ didn't listen to him. From within his exile he wept and addressed words to the city that were heard only by the leaves and hornets: '*O if only you knew, and on this very day, what is in the interests of your peace . . . But you didn't notice the day when you were visited.*'

WHEN?

'*There'll come a time when a stone won't remain on a stone . . .*'

Not from Satan, but from the angry wisdom of God. Not spitting and curses but a more terrifying vengeance fell on the city from the lips of the rejected one. The prophecy of the end. Jerusalem, the world, me – we're one single thing, a thing condemned to perish and our punishment is this description uttered by Christ to Peter, John and Andrew on the Mount of Olives. I've only to open the book at the thirteenth chapter of Mark. It's about that lucid and powerful delirium in which I'm told what will happen to the city where I live, to my friends, to the cells within which I breathe.

And I know that from now onwards *peoples will be seen rising against peoples and kingdoms against kingdoms; there will be plagues, famines, and extraordinary signs in the skies. And this will be no more than the beginning of the suffering.* I know that *brothers will put brothers to death, fathers will kill sons, and sons will rebel against their parents and put them to death.* I know that my city where I could walk with my eyes shut because the streets are so familiar to me by their smell *will be laid low by the pagans* and the inhabitants of my quarter who greet me friendlily *will be put to the sword and taken away as slaves.* Among the roofs and chimneys familiar to me *the sun will grow dark, the moon will no longer give its light and the stars will fall from the firmament,* and in my land like everywhere
146

else, *nations will be a prey to anguish and wonder what's to happen in that uproar of wild seas and waves.*

And as the mark of Christ is on me despite my betrayals and blasphemies, I know that *before these things happen they'll get hold of me, cast me into tribulation, consign me to prison, drag me before the law courts and scourge me in the synagogues;* because that day he also said: '*You'll be hated because of my name.*'

That hour will come. And if, owing to my instinct for self-preservation, I try to use my imagination and take precautions about what to do, the answer is: nothing. *Whoever's on the roof shouldn't go down into the house, or go home to get anything, and whoever's in the fields shouldn't go back to fetch his coat.*

So I must remain stuck where I am, not run home, not get up from the writing-desk to see whether my children are at home or in some hell where they're being swallowed up in a crumbling city.

I know there'll be no pity for anyone. No safe-conducts, no privileges in the name of youth and innocence. *And woe to pregnant women or those who have a baby at the breast in those days! Pray that you haven't to flee in winter* . . . Perhaps I'll see my son's pregnant wife struggling in that universal trap, and my daughter's babies clinging to her breasts.

When we hear that drumbeat of prophecies, there's only one word we can crouch behind, as behind a rock. 'When, when will all that happen, Lord?' But the answer is both full of pity and inexorable: *As for the day and the hour, no one knows, not even the angels in heaven, nor the Son, but only the Father.*

All we know is that on that day the inscrutable justice of the Father will cut destiny from destiny like a hatchet. *Then two will be in the same field and one will be taken and the other left. Two women will be grinding corn; one will be taken and the other left. On that night two people will be in the same bed; one will be taken away, the other left.*

We ask *when*, and he answers with a warning both harsh and passionate: *that day will come on you unexpectedly like a snare* . . . ; and he tells us that the catastrophe could come in our own time: *just as in the days before the flood people ate and drank, married husbands and wives, until the day Noah went into the ark, and nobody*

147

noticed anything until the flood came and carried them all away, so it will be when the Son of man comes.

When! In fact the answer isn't difficult, indeed approximatively it's easy. Not for thousands of years, no, as our thirst for time and life would like to predict. In the hour of my death. My death will be all these things simply because it'll be my end, and I know that as far as I'm concerned a stone won't be left on a stone.

In that hour the mountains and stars will declare war on me, all my faults will become a cliff that collapses on top of me, every evil thought a moon that falls headlong onto my head, all the wrongly-enjoyed women will become whales and sea-monsters vomited on me as I agonize in the horrible mixture of ocean and land. My death will be easily recognized in the roof from which it's not worth descending, the field in which you don't turn back, the coat it's not worth going to fetch, the bed in which one person will be left and the other taken. It will be that *great earthquake,* that *uproar of wild seas and waves,* even if it happens beneath a quiet canopy with my family around me.

On that day Christ predicted all this for me: he anticipated my death in the form of a human and physical Jerusalem. Why was it so terrifying? Perhaps this is simply another act of mercy – Christ's alienation in me because he can't save us or spare us the tragedy except by becoming one in us? I mean perhaps he wanted to join us in our madness and this monologue is nothing more than a delirium of mine taken over by Jesus and carried to his calvary of words and terrors? In that case, once we have raised our eyes from his inhumane discourse (seeing that all our love of life and hope resides in him) we hope to wish that Christ will burn up all this horror in his imagining: and that *it will not be,* and never should be, true – precisely because, *by putting it into words,* this catastrophe of ours is burnt out in his own mouth; we wish to hope that as the Saviour died for everyone, so he alone has passed through this agony in our stead.

If the Lord hadn't shortened those days, no one would have been saved; but he cut them short for the sake of the elect he had forechosen . . .
I know I'm not one of the elect who'll placate God's tempest:
148

but I can go out of my house and run and kiss the hand of a good old man who lives in a nearby convent.

But not a hair of your head will perish. You'll save your souls by your patience; and I warm myself at the ray of kindness that breaks through the darkness of that apocalyptic discourse. I reread the words of light on this page, the ones written with the whiteness of clouds, that promise his presence with us in the panic of that moment: *Then the Son of man will appear in the sky . . . they'll see him arriving on the clouds with great power and glory,* and he'll be *like lightning which flashes from one extremity of the heavens to the other* . . . And I tell myself that those will be the signs of his return among us. Why should I be afraid?

CARNIVAL AT JERUSALEM

When he was near the descent of the Mount of Olives the whole crowd of disciples began praising the Lord with great shouts of joy because of all the miracles they'd seen . . .

Just occasionally a period like this falls on our earth: a period of hosannas. Jerusalem's enthusiastic cry to Christ as he entered through its walls. On such occasions another miracle bursts out here below: the miracle of gratitude. In order to be grateful people need an interior miracle, they need to contradict their natures – by flying or, like Peter, by walking on the water of the lake. They need to be intoxicated by a superhuman wine. Then the day-to-day law – of resentment against anyone who has done us a kindness, of sarcasm against anyone good – is broken. Men's gratitude isn't love: it's something else – it's the animal-like yet tender fanaticism of someone who clings to the favour bestowed; a sort of mechanical love of give and take, but for that very reason more human, and consuming like a fever. It doesn't last long: just long enough to unburden on the benefactor the quasi-rebellious emotion of our indebtedness. The human race holds inequalities, that is to say obvious debts, in horror. The hosannas and blessings of that Jewish crowd were almost a counter-attack on a dictator of favours, the

149

lynching of a monster of kindness, so as to re-establish an equilibrium and exorcize a power it was difficult to bear. Man's gratitude doesn't go out to others for what they *are* (as Mary of Bethany loved Jesus when she sat at his feet), but for what they *give*. In this case they loved him in so far as they were certain that he would give more, the Kingdom: *Blessed is the king of Israel, blessed is the kingdom that comes from our father David* . . . Behind the red tunic of this prophet there flapped the old dream of glory and revenge, armies, booty, Jewish fleets entering the Roman seas with sails unfurled.

Jesus advanced on the back of a colt *on which no one had ever ridden*. Humble little creature, hosanna to you too, the last of the gospel animals, omega to that alpha which thirty years earlier carried the baby Christ into Egypt. They covered its back with a cloak so that Jesus should have a soft saddle, and beneath its feet they spread other cloaks so that those muddy hooves should tread on silk and purple when in the saddle there sat *he who comes in the name of the Lord*. And now that they had removed their cloaks so as to spread them on the ground, the men gathered round the colt and the master who bestrode it were no longer men, or no longer whole men. For in the frenetic waving of palms there were legs of nimble cripples, blind men's eyes whose shell of darkness had been broken open, fingers and noses which had sprouted anew on the scabs of leprosy, the jars of Cana filled with vintage wine, the loaves and fishes begotten in the desert on that hungry day; while on the ground, shattered and quivering like relics, lay the withered hand, the blood of the woman with the haemorrhage, the hump of the little old woman, the squint-eyed spectres of the possessed. And there was the dead boy from Nain, Jairus's daughter, and Lazarus, all living and happy in their mortal remains. It wasn't the people miraculously cured, but the bits and pieces of their miracles that welcomed Christ that day in his brief earthly carnival. Hosanna, blessed . . .

I'm not interested that within six days that same crowd, swept along in the frenzy of the corrida, should have wanted Christ dead, should have yelled that he must be crucified, and should have opted for the murderer Barabbas to cherish like a baby in his stead. Those truncated bits, those broken things would not betray him, they would climb with him gropingly to the cross. And they would go on crying hosanna every day till the end of the world; even now they are dancing round us, and we trip up over them, we bawlers of Jerusalem.

THE PASSION

He began to be afraid and sorrowful.

AS LONG AS WE CAN STAND IT

'I passionately wanted to eat with you this Passover.'

He only needed to breathe on the world. Sin, that iron barrier between men and love, would have dissolved like a dandelion-clock blown away by children. On that day the world would have come to itself again, as an epileptic emerges from a fit and smiles at the passers-by who have helped him.

He only needed to breathe. But he preferred things the way he said he wanted them. *'I passionately wanted to eat with you this Passover.'* Not the tasty meat of lamb nor the delights of a long-drawn-out meal with friends; no – his passionate desire was to have himself eaten, to put himself in the place of the lamb. And in order to be eaten he had first to have his throat cut and be emptied of all his blood. He maintained there was no other way by which we'd realize what he felt for us and remember him till the end of time. This phrase surely belonged to him more totally than many uttered in the past three years, and it seemed an affectionate way of saying: *'There's no greater love than to lay down one's life for one's friends.'*

As for us, we're repelled by his passion, either because we love him so much or because of our horror of blood and death. But we can't tell him this. When Peter rebelled on hearing that the Master would be tortured to death, he elicited Christ's bitterest rebuke: *'Get away from me, Satan . . .'*

So into the human family already loaded with sorrows he preferred to bring a new sorrow – his death, a final remorse, his massacre on the hill.

How can we be grateful to him for this choice, the most tragic among the thousand possible choices he had for our salvation? The point is that Christ doesn't ask for our gratitude, nor for our tears. He doesn't even ask us to understand. And he certainly doesn't ask us to lash ourselves out of remorse for our direct co-responsibility, as some devotional teachers would have us do: my selfishnesses are the hammer-blows, my debaucheries stripped him on Calvary. He asks us to drink of the mystery of his choice simply because we mysteriously love him – as he drank of the cup in the garden; he asks us to see the sorrow and death that daily consume us in terms of that Friday – as falling to sleep with our head on his breast; he asks us to follow his passion step by step without even understanding it. We can't play the part of John who went all the way to the foot of the cross, but in those last pages there's an unnamed person in whom we may see ourselves: *A young man followed him wearing only a linen shirt, and when they laid hands on him he left the linen shirt in their hands and ran away naked.*

Let's follow him as long as we can stand it. Then we'll leave our shirt in the torturers' hands and escape to some place the gospel doesn't mention.

FROM BELOW

And with the knowledge that his time had come to pass from this world to the Father . . . he poured water into a bowl and began washing his disciples' feet.

His time had come. And his first action following the fateful blow on the gong – in a rite that seemed prearranged – was to go and fetch a bowl. The gospel makes us feel that this logic is obvious, this consequence expressed in a tight circle of grammar: with the knowledge that his time had come, he began to . . .

What did he begin doing in the cenacle when he knew he had to die? In what direction flew his first almost automatic act of obedience to the dark message? He rose from the table, tore himself from the comforts of a delightful rest, and washed feet.

What should a man do who knows he's shortly to die? If he loves someone and has something to leave, he makes his will. In our case we ask for pen and paper. Christ went and fetched a bowl and a towel and poured water into the receptacle. The will starts here; and here, with the last foot dried, it could well finish. Bent over a sheet of paper we write: 'I bequeath my house, my land, to . . .' Jesus, bent over a bowl of water, removed the dirt from the feet of his friends. In the silence of the room the careful washing lasted a long time, and the breathing of the kneeling man became rather heavier as the minutes passed, and his hair fell over his forehead.

Christ was at his work, on the same level as the dogs gnawing at the lamb's last bare bone under the table and interrupting their Easter supper to marvel at that man on all fours like themselves. Yes, he chose to begin saving us from below. In the final picture he would dominate us from above, from the bloody beam, with arms outstretched ('*When I'm raised up I'll draw the whole world to myself*'). But the first scene was this one: crouching like an animal over our toes, over our unpoetic nails, over those unattractive odours. He permitted himself the royal joy of self-humiliation.

How could he have loved our feet? Under some aspects, Lord, the stuff we're made of isn't at all unpleasant – we even have beautiful and lovable parts. Philip had the profile of a gay bird, John the wide gentle eyes of a boy; but at the level you chose there's no friendship or agreeable relationship. Feet are miles away from their possessors' smiles, feet are rough wild animals, and looking at a foot makes it harder to believe in man's soul and easier to think we're just transitory puppets whose destiny is dissolution. Perhaps that's why the dead are all feet, they stick them out in front of them without any shame at all. And perhaps that's why the living hide these protuberances with a kind of instinctive modesty. As Peter said: '*You'll never wash my feet!*' O fisherman, it wasn't your zealous determination not to be done a service that made you cry out in protest, it was deep-seated: our feet, even if they can give a caress, even if they can make history with their ever-hopeful

154

forward march, are dirty and ridiculous. Only our mothers could handle our feet without disgust.

And yet . . . it's precisely through surrendering all our pride to the hands of Christ-as-mother, through identifying him bent over the bowl with her when she scrubbed us clean, that our salvation must pass. *'If I don't wash you, you'll have no part with me.'*

Let's all become mothers, creatures with no feelings of revulsion; because in Christ there's the mother-figure (as well as the master) and it's only by taking her as our example – just as it's only by becoming children again – that the Kingdom can become a reality.

'Do you understand what I've done to you? You call me Lord and Master, and you do so rightly, because I am. So if I've washed your feet for you, you should wash each other's feet. I've given you the example, so that you too will do what I've done.'

I've given you the example . . . If I had to choose some relic of the passion, I wouldn't pick up a scourge or a spear but that round bowl of dirty water. To go round the world with that receptacle under my arm, looking only at people's feet; and for each one I'd tie a towel round me, bend down, and never raise my eyes higher than their ankles, so as not to distinguish friends from enemies. I'd wash the feet of atheists, drug-addicts, arms-dealers, the murderer of the boy in the rushes, the pimp profiteering from back-street prostitutes, the suicide – and all in silence: until they'd understood.

I haven't the gift of turning myself into bread and wine, of sweating blood, of enduring thorns and nails. *My* passion, my imitation of Jesus when he was about to die can stop here.

THE HIDING-PLACE

'Take it and eat it: this is my body . . .'

Everything, including the consecration, was foreseen and written; I know that. But even in Christ the man there's a fantastic and emotional psychology which surprised even

155

himself, and which in the freedom of improvisation was to coincide in a mystical way with the eternal will of the Father. At this point I see his eyes wandering around over the remains of the bread on the table-cloth, and then shining with an ineffable inspiration: this, this would be his hiding-place. That's where he would take refuge. That night they wouldn't capture him in his entirety; they'd think they'd done so, they'd think they'd dragged him away from his companions, yet really they would scourge and crucify a ghost: he had hidden himself in that bread. Rather as in Galilee, when they wanted to seize him and kill him or make him king, he had the knack of hiding himself and disappearing from sight. So he stretched out his hand over the already broken bread, broke it into smaller bits and, raising it into the air, pronounced the words of the magic transition: '*This is my body, it's been given for you.*'

. . . no, it wasn't so as to escape the lance-thrusts. All his flesh – not a ghost – was there for the executioners to tear at within a few hours. But the hiding-place was still valid, and by inventing it in that instant he really did leave to his followers a Christ that no one could ferret out and wrench from their hands. Let them eat him. Let their breast become the hiding-place of a hiding-place. A little earlier Jesus had washed their feet, he'd besmirched himself with the muddiest part of their physical being. Now he wanted to do more: he wanted to go down their throats, mix himself with their mucous membranes to the point of transforming himself, and gradually melt into all the fibres of their body.

The primary significance of the eucharist isn't mystical but physical, almost a clinging to the material being of his friends who would stay on and live. He said 'This is my body' with a tenderness that first and foremost exalted it itself. Not 'This is my spirit' or 'This is generalized goodness or well-being' – possibly they wouldn't have known what to do with such things. It was necessary to them that he should remain with the only thing we really know and attach our hearts and memories to – the body; and that it should be a desirable, acceptable and homely body. That's why he looked over that table-cloth for the easiest, most familiar and most concrete thing: bread. So as to quench hunger and give pleasure. Above all so as to stay. That evening Christ measured out for us all the millions of evenings before we'd see him face to face; he measured out the long separation. He knew that men forget things within a few days, that distance destroys things, that it's useless for lovers to insert a lock of hair in letters that are going far away across land and sea. If Peter himself, and John and Andrew and James would forget, then in order that their children and their grandchildren's children shouldn't forget he had to throw between himself and me that never-ending bridge of bread. *'Do this in memory of me.'*

'. . . it's shed for you . . .'

But in the cup that he raised immediately afterwards there lies something else – another sign. No more escape almost unharmed, under cover of his companions. The wine was blood; and blood in itself, outside the body, signifies violence and tragedy. To extract that blood, jabs of steel and hate would be required, it would shoot out in pain from his body, death would follow pain, and all this would be the passion. It rebounded in the exact measure of the debt that had to be paid, the stain that had to be washed away: *'This is the cup of my blood shed for you for the remission of sins.'*

We've no means of discovering the relationship between sin and blood, between sin and drinking from that cup. But his recommendation was peremptory and heart-felt: *'All of you, drink.'* As if it was only by drinking what spurted from his wounds that we could prevent him from dying of bloodlessness, prevent the precious liquid being lost among nettles and stones on the ground. As if by swallowing that juice pressed from his suffering, life and joy and the colour of his cheeks would come back to the world, and his life among us on earth, instead of closing, would start again on a golden Christmas night.

All drank of it, writes the evangelist. And then they realized that the supper really was over, because that wine no longer tasted like wine.

ONE OF US

'It would be better if he'd never been born.'

Supper had begun – before he washed their feet – on a sombre note of good-bye. Jesus had passed a cup to his disciples: *'Take it and divide it among you,'* he'd said; *'as for me I tell you I won't be drinking any more of the fruit of the vine until the kingdom of God has come.'* Yet on reading the opening phrases of the agape we don't get the impression that the climax of the impending tragedy had in any way gathered momentum over the heads of the twelve apostles. To begin with there was that silly and inappropriate discussion – halfway between a joke and a piece of malicious vanity – about which of them should be considered the most important and sit nearest the Master. Then the supper, the fragrant smell and taste of the food, the delicious gulps of wine, opened the way to the quiet waters of concrete euphoria and exorcizing magic. Lamb, good bread, good wine, the first stains on the table-cloth and the eyes of his companions becoming brighter and more cordial. Eating together is important, nothing engenders more courage about life and more carefreeness about death. Perhaps that phrase – 'I won't be drinking any more of the fruit of the vine' – had been just another of his intellectual metaphors. And besides, what did he mean by 'until the kingdom of God has come'? They'd never really understood very clearly what the 'kingdom' was, and for all they knew it might appear beneath their feet tomorrow as ever was – all green with vineyards.

Anyone spying in through one of the windows would have thought that no place on earth was sweeter than that cenacle, no harmony more enviable than in that group in the gathering darkness, no greater brotherly gentleness than in those young friends assembled round the table as in some safe haven. One of them was leaning his head on the breast of the greatest of them and appeared to be dreaming. No other confraternity could have seemed so removed from hatred and threats; memories hovered around them, and outside the crickets were chirruping among the prickly pears. That was the Kingdom: what else could it be but that Easter rejoicing, that drinking to the full of the cup into which he first had dipped his lips? Their eyes were closed or wide-open on rosy mirages when there flowed over them the gentlest phrase that had ever caressed them: '. . . *you're the people who've always stayed beside me in my ordeals and I'm preparing a kingdom for you* . . .' O Master, what you're saying is even more beautiful than when you washed everyone's feet a short while ago.

But suddenly, without changing his tone, Jesus added: '*One of you will betray me, one of you now eating with me* . . .' The storm had been set in motion. From this moment – while the other chickens were nestled under the hen within – one was outside in the cold. One man was lost; and even if he was the only one, that destiny plunged into perdition, that truncated creature is the tragedy of creation and immensely more serious than all the wars and lamentations of our history since Adam.

. . . they began asking him which of them it was, and each started saying: 'Could it be me?'
They would rise from the table with their anguish unresolved, with the question still there – which had been addressed not so much to him as by each one to himself. Each of them looked with bated breath at his own hands on the table, for he had added (though without a hostile glance or a trace of bitterness in his voice): '*The hand of the man who's betraying me is with me here on the table.*' Each looked at his chest and arms and wondered whether his body was the body of the man who . . . *it were better had never been born.* None of them really knew themselves so they suspected they were capable of anything; they realized that even on this cherished night the very climax of faithfulness to their idolized companion could fall headlong into crime; the ill-will, doubt and secret rancour which in the last three years had poisoned their hearts against the Master at least once, now made them turn pale – eleven Judases sharing the pallor of the real Judas. 'Could it be me?'

Only one of them had his doubts dissolved immediately and

his peace of mind restored. This was John, the young apostle *whom Jesus loved.* 'Lord, *who is it?*' He breathed his question because as he spoke he was leaning on Jesus' breast. With John perhaps the question didn't arise from his own inner anxiety for he addressed it to Christ under the raving gesticulations of Peter who caught his eye (*Simon Peter made a sign and asked him,* '*Who are you talking about?*'). And the answer was heard only by John who was the nearest: '*It's the one to whom I'll offer a piece of soaked bread.*'

Christ's hand dipped the bread and stretched without a tremor towards the plate of a man on his left. O hand, stop! This was a gesture of charm and goodwill at banquets in Palestine. But you must drop the bread; continue your journey but grab the black forelock of Simon Iscariot's son, and drag, drag that head down onto the other half of your breast, the half not taken up by John, so that the hair of the loved one and that of the cursed one shall mingle. Then stroke his neck with some rough gesture as you would a great unfaithful dog. And in his ear just whisper the name – Judas: the name which from this moment will become a curse for centuries unless you utter it with your voice so as to hold him back from taking that step.

But on went the piece of bread, and down onto the plate. Bread had to play the leading part that evening: bread and wine. Before instituting the eucharist of life, Christ instituted that eucharist of condemnation and death. The man on his left chewed and swallowed. And, as the evangelist puts it, Satan *entered into him.* His friends thought that with that gesture of goodwill the Master intended to relieve Judas from the suspicion of being the traitor. When they saw him hurrying out, and when Jesus whispered his command: '*Do what you're doing quickly*', they thought Judas was going to buy something for the communal feast.

John's head, the head *that knew*, remained on Jesus' heart while the ten went on anxiously pondering their question: 'Could it be me?' And I go on pondering my question: Why wasn't Judas's head on Jesus' heart? He was sitting near him, he had hair to be ruffled, a name to be called by. I don't understand that the strength required for withholding that

160

embrace was a superhuman strength, equal to the miracle of the raising of Lazarus. I don't understand that in him there was and had to be a tremendous and mysterious diversity.

Then Judas hurried out. And it was night.
Now, and from now onwards, it wasn't he who did what he did; it wasn't Simon Iscariot's son who entered the garden with a clicking of footsteps, among torches, bringing soldiers with him; who accosted Jesus and kissed him; it was the other, the one who had entered into him through his mouth with the dipped bread and would henceforth push him and pull him like a herd of cattle.

Satan entered into Judas not in the days of the intrigue, when as keeper of the purse he plotted with the elders of the Sanhedrin to sell his master for thirty pieces of silver; but in that very subtle interplay of passions, in that vertiginous moment there in the cenacle (*'Could it be me?' 'You've said it'*) when all was still open to destiny. When, in that instant of time, through a tragic choice of the blood, baseness had closed all his pores to love, had dimmed in his eyes the faces of his friends round the table, had dissolved in his nostrils the odour of those bodies and those dishes, and had shattered the sweet power of the things around him. It was then that Satan – the being without memory or hope – erupted into him with his great courage. Satan put that courage in the place of puppet-Judas's bewilderment, and with that courage inside him Judas got up, opened the door, closed it behind him, and went out into the night. The night neither frightened him nor allured him, it hardly gave him the sense that it was absorbing into itself his outline as a man. Because he was now the same substance as the night.

And yet Judas isn't quite so tragically simple for us, he isn't just the blind herd, the empty puppet, the lone oak up there in the mountains struck by theological lightning. Judas was a man as I'm a man. No worse, no more of a sinner than me. (What does betrayal mean? All it means is *not understanding, not being* the other; it means being, as we are, someone living as an exile within himself and betraying all others at every moment.) What *was* his sin, that betrayal that has made him the symbol of infamy over the centuries? A mean little sin of greed and confusion, the sin of a poor wretched fellow with small ambitions and megalomaniac dreams. Like Satan, Mary, the apostles and so many others, he didn't grasp who Christ was, he didn't foresee that his betrayal would cost the life of the redeemer of the world.

There are plenty of Judases who steal away in the shadow of the night and don't turn round out of fear that the lights from the cenacle will suck them back again, as the moon draws back the tide from the shores. There's the metaphysical Judas who's a mysterious symbol, an enigma. A Judas who, by the power of paradox, turns into a religious figure (hasn't someone said that for Judas the betrayal of Christ was perhaps the only way he could bind himself to him for all eternity – a mad outburst of love?). But there's the other Judas, my brother in body and breath, who began like me as a foetus in a woman's belly, then grew up, unable to stay put in a child's skin, amid blows and fevers and frightened nights, coughing nights. There's the man who felt such horror at the sight of his first corpse or united himself in wonderment with the first woman who came along hoping that in that enchantment lay the answer to the terror of living; who fell asleep every evening for thousands of evenings mingling the innocent memories of childhood with beguiling calculations about a better tomorrow (there flashed through his mind, little Jewish urchin as he was, the glory of a kingdom where he'd be a minister).

How many Judases have run out into the night since that Thursday of the passion! A Chinese ghost without body or feeling, a bogey-man, a werewolf howling among sleeping houses. Or the docile holy executant of a superhuman command – the hardest and most frightening; the man who, like Christ, would have liked to say to an angel who never visited him: 'If it's possible, take this cup away from me'? Judas is the knot and nodal point of all that, and it's not for us to untie it. It wasn't possible to stop him and embrace him that night because Judas no longer had body or arms. It would have been vain to talk to him because he hadn't ears, and vain too to appeal to him because he no longer had feelings: he was the pure unconscious of all of us walking around and suffering, he was the torment of our nightmares and our lusts which had coagulated in him, and it was he who bore them. His cross had no shape, it was the weight of existence itself, it was the movement within us of a swarming tangle of monsters.

Alone Judas went through his passion which had few stages, but loathsome and hallucinating ones. The rendezvous with the squad of soldiers waiting for him, the kiss on Christ's cheek; then the dash to the sanctuary, the heated dialogue with the elders ('*I've betrayed innocent blood.*' '*What do we care?*'), the clatter of the thirty pieces of silver scattered on the ground. And then the rope, the fig-tree, the lonely bursting of his bowels – he and his two hands at his throat – the quick suffocation to stifle remorse. In comparison Jesus' cross, with all those people coming and going, the daylight, the cursing, the blessing, the weeping, was a festival of colour and life. It wasn't death, and Christ was to rise again. Only Judas's death was death.

THE LONG GOOD-BYE

'*You don't any of you ask me: "Where are you going?"*'

Supper was over. Everything was finished – the food, the actions, the gestures. Judas had betrayed; Jesus had transformed the bread and wine.

So now he took leave of his companions. He didn't kiss them one by one and he didn't call them by their names. He had a long thing to say and he said it. He knew it wasn't because of his miracles that they'd followed him. He well remembered Peter's answer when he asked: '*Do you want to go away too?*' '*Lord, to whom shall we go? Only you have the words of eternal life.*'

Words. His last: the most bewitched by eternity, so that they would stay with them even afterwards, and with their children, and with the children of their children, for thousands of years.

He didn't kiss them. The first syllables he uttered bound him

163

to the eleven far more than any human embrace: '*I'm the vine and you're the branches.*' Pointless to put their arms round each other – separation was henceforth out of the question. '*Whoever lives in me, and I in him, produces plenty of fruit because without me you can do nothing.*' Think of the beatitude of this statement – hearing their powerlessness proclaimed. Nothing . . . What else, except his voice that night, could transform such a mortifying pronouncement into something so voluptuous?

But what could they do if they were capable of nothing? Listen, as they were now doing: mute and enraptured in the reflection of the torches flickering on their faces. Listen to their instructions: '*You are my friends if you do what I command you . . .*', '*This is my commandment: love one another as I've loved you . . .*'

He told them they weren't servants; rather, he called them friends; but on this occasion he didn't exhort them as one does with friends, he gave them inflexible commands like servants: '*This is my commandment,*' he began again, '*love one another.*'

Of course they'd love one another; they already loved one another – all round a table when it's dark outside as it was now and each providing warm memories for the others, what was easier, what sweeter? '*No one*', the voice went on, '*has greater love than the man who lays down his life for his friends.*'

Then he went on about hate. '*If the world hates you, realize that it hated me before you.*' '*It's because you aren't of the world, that's why the world hates you.*' '*They hated me without reason.*'

But suddenly his words became wilder and more mysterious. He'd hardly announced persecution and tragedy for all ('*They'll drive you from the synagogues, and people who kill you will think they're honouring God*'), he'd hardly said, '*Now I'm going . . .*', when an unforeseeable, strange and scandalous pronouncement issued from his implacable lips. A pronouncement corresponding to no object, not even to a feeling unless it was some ancient repudiated longing, a child's broken toy. Nor was it really a pronouncement, it was rather as if he'd ceased to speak and had struck an unknown cymbal: '*I'll tell you the truth, you'll weep and groan; and meanwhile the world will rejoice: you'll be sad, but your sadness will turn into joy.*' '*When a woman gives birth to a child she feels pain because her hour has come, but once the baby is born she doesn't remember the birth-pains because of her joy that a human being has been born into the world.' 'So now you're sad, but I'll see you again and your hearts will rejoice, and no one will take your joy away from you.' 'So far you haven't asked anything in my name: ask and you shall obtain it and your joy will be complete.'*

'Joy?' whispered those hard-bitten men to each other, 'Joy? ... What animal is that, Lord? We can't remember it any more and we didn't want to give it another thought. Or perhaps it's a whore you're allowing us to sleep with? Or a smell?' So Christ explained; it seemed to be someone who'd come among them later, someone with a peculiar name: *'It's better for you that I should go, because if I don't go the Paraclete won't come among you; but if I go I'll send him to you . . .'*

He was about to undergo the most horrible and painful ordeal that a man has ever had to endure, and he was talking of joy. *'I've told you this so that you'll have peace in me. You'll have tribulation in the world, but trust in me: I've overcome the world.'* If the world had been overcome, was this phrase still permissible, and were miracles still possible?

He was still talking, his elbows on the table and with longer and longer pauses. But now he was raising his eyes upwards and wasn't talking with *them* any more though he was talking *about* them. And they couldn't understand his divine delirium. Christ's monologue came to them broken and confused like the buzzing of a bee that's now flying about, now perched somewhere or other, now out of sight. They felt he was still talking about joy, glory, the world. They felt – and this held their attention as they struggled with the torpors of wine and the onset of sleep – that he was still talking about them: *'They were yours and you gave them to me . . . I pray for them, for those you've given me, because they're yours . . . From now on I'm no longer in the world, but they're still in the world . . . I don't ask you to take them from the world but to protect them from harm . . . I'd like those you've given me to be with me wherever I am . . . I'm not praying only for them but also for those who'll believe in me, by their word, so that all may be one and the same: as you, Father, are in me and I'm in you . . .'*

Words escaping all meaning, for them and for us, and escaping from this man's lips like notes from an ivory horn playing by itself in a valley where all the huntsmen are dead. Christ was already in the Father, and the Father was a land too mysterious and distant. That's why no one asked him, 'Where are you going?' and no one made any further effort to follow him. It's enough for us, as for his friends, to stay crouching and silent round the table and hear those abstruse words trembling with the hope that he repeated more than once that night: '*A short time and you won't see me, and then another short time and you will see me . . .*'

SILENCE

He began to be frightened and sad.

That night in the garden he asked for something for the first time. He asked the three dearest to him to '*stay and keep awake with me*'. That small thing was enough – that Peter, John and James should stay there silently sitting on the roots of an old olive tree and bear a little of the night's vapours with him while he prayed. It didn't matter if they didn't pray because it was cold. Just to know that they were a few feet away, and awake. '*Keep awake with me . . .*'

The response to this request – all that his friends could offer him – was silence interrupted by a faint snore. They had removed themselves in the only way they could without actually fleeing – in the cowardly and innocent way of sleep. If those three had stayed awake with him – composing as they did the last threads Jesus held to prevent him sinking into horror – he would have been spared the most terrifying part of the passion; it would have been enough to hear them breathing, clearing their throats from time to time, or rubbing their sandals on the ground. Or perhaps he would have talked again, as in the cenacle, and the living forest of words would have acted as a screen against the image of death. But sleep cut off the three last threads that bound Christ to the land of his earthly brothers.

Then he called on the Father: '*Father, if it's possible, take this cup away from me.*' Three times he made this appeal. Of course it was still *possible*. It was at the very last moment that the Father had stayed the knife held over the boy Isaac and opened the door to a happy ending for Abraham, as in a fairy story. And he was appealing to the Father after thirty years' experience of fathers and sons on earth, of their love for each other and of their wanting each other to live. But on this night the Father's silence was smooth and dense like the very essence of the world. The Father had answered his prayer at the tomb of Lazarus and raised a man who'd been dead four days. For the first time the silence was a surprise even to Jesus.

We're all aware of that final silence that lies at the bottom of our prayers, when we've made an invocation and then we hold our breath and listen . . . and there's nothing. There follows, as it did for you, the desire to annihilate ourselves. *He threw himself down with his face to the ground.* The ground, the black or grey ground that holds us up is the drum on which we clamour for help, the mother in whom we're swallowed up so as to rush back to our origins as animals crouching in a belly. But the ground against which Christ pressed his face had no maternal complicity with him. It was just a stretch of garden, clay and little ferns brown in the dusk and some nocturnal insect flying about. The ground was his last frontier now that he couldn't see houses or trees or other tall things; but a frontier that would remain closed, even if he called on it to open and become nothingness. No, alas, nothingness doesn't exist, Lord; your Father couldn't create it; only a man like me or you – at an hour like this – longs for it and adores it with his desperate imagination. Nothingness is the paradise forbidden to us.

And this was your passion, Christ, when with your face against the roots you went through the metaphysical anguish of us all. Here your soul was on the cross like that of all our brothers who on some night or other lose their faith. With their twisted arms the olive trees of Gethsemane became fantastic monsters, symbols of all that is for ever foreign to us; yet at the same time they suddenly become confessors of our new sin – the sin of fear and boredom and the disheartened acceptance that everything finishes with death. In their neutral existence, do trees *know*? And is it possible that from their bark the oracle can emerge that may solve the enigma?

His face, as the evangelist puts it, was covered *with a sweat like drops of blood*, and Christ finally wept between two longings. There was the life within himself and around himself that he would have liked to make lasting because as a man he had tasted its delights – he knew now that everything in it was sweet, even the persecution of the Pharisees – whereas soon they would wrest life from his body and his glassy eyes would no longer see the hills or the clouds or the spear with which Longinus would pierce his heart. And then there was his other longing, heaven, the Father: but what if in the meanwhile his Father had died? . . .

So his hour went on, eternal in the shadows of the garden and swinging between the two fateful silences. That of men (*'Why are you asleep? Couldn't you have stayed awake with me for an hour?'* Then he went back again to the disciples and found them again asleep . . . and they couldn't even answer him*). And that of the Father ('. . . *for you everything is possible!*'), who was now hiding only in the little trembling fern and in the insect nestling among the blades of grass.

SLEEP

He came to the disciples who had fallen asleep in their sadness, and he said to them : 'Why are you sleeping?'

PETER: Who's that? Who are you? Is it you already? You dog, are you one of those who want to kill my master? Wake up, friends: a sword. Death. Who's talking of death? It's you who'll get death. We'll get the Kingdom, Judas's kingdom with its big blond king, you won't dare to raise a hand against him, because I . . .

Master, was it you? . . . Forgive me. So they aren't here yet. What made me fall asleep? Sleep's a traitor, like Judas.

James, John . . . It's your fault. I told you to shake me if I dozed off.

So you're alive, Master, thank God. Never fear. We're here. And thank you for waking me up. I was in the middle of an appalling nightmare. I dreamt of a thousand spears. And then that people were crucifying me, upside down.

JAMES: No, don't wake me. Why's your hand shaking me? Let me sleep. I don't know whose hand it is or what wrist and shoulder it's attached to. And I don't care. Tonight I've neither friends nor enemies, neither duties nor engagements. This sleep has set me free at last: from the Master and the other disciples, from my wife and children I left behind so as to follow a man about whom I can't remember a thing except that he had a red cloak. The only friend I've got is this foam of sleep – no memories, no worries, just sweet oblivion in the depths of my body. All I love is this soft cushion of turf which I chose for resting my cheek on and shutting my eyes, the warm coat I threw over my legs and then stole from the other two with whom I was sharing it – I can't remember their names.

JOHN: Lord, I don't know about them, but I fell asleep out of sadness.

One day you put us on this earth and forbade us to kill ourselves. It's not given to us to escape from our great prison. But in your goodness you did leave us sleep, that land where even we poor people can find refuge – when we haven't money to get on a boat we can at least close our eyes.

That's where I was. And the garden and Judas and the soldiers who'll soon be here weren't there, they didn't even know. You were there. And my dead mother. And we three were alive and together. You didn't work any miracles – everyone was happy and well. You'd even given up the Kingdom. My mother looked after the house. After supper for hours on end and with no one disturbing us you told us your parables. I rested my head on your heart and listened to you with my eyes closed.

Only now that you've woken me up do I see that it wasn't you but Peter's back. Please forgive me.

WITHOUT WINGS OR TRUMPET

An angel appeared to him.

Jesus, where are you? Like one of these olives fallen to the ground, have you got crushed in the olive-press of too terrible an ordeal? Whom will the soldiers find when they come, as they soon will, to start the passion on which my salvation depends? But there's his shadow standing erect and his voice is once more that of the Lord of all destinies. *'That's enough, the hour has come . . . Get up, let's go.'* Someone had been with him, he'd overcome the demon of the black trees, the pettiness of life and death.

Who was that angel, what was he and where did he come from – that power of consolation over the man who was more dead than this or any other night? The biographer gives us only eight words: *an angel appeared to him to comfort him.* And he couldn't say more because this last angel in Christ's life had no wings or trumpet or halo, he was and is quite invisible and has no words to say to us that aren't ours already and reposing within us. That angel was no more than an immortal pity who wings through creation and comes at the last moment; unable to make us conquer our despair, he carries us beyond it.

The angel in the garden was that part of us that is our own mother and sister, a submerged courage, perhaps the cry of all our memories, perhaps just the scent of hay at night which restores heaven and earth to us. It isn't hard to believe in angels of this sort. They're us ourselves and yet they're someone else: an unexpected messenger from the mute Father.

THE FIRST WOUND

And he kissed him.

Perhaps the secret angel who performed the miracle of raising him beyond fear did no more than kiss him. When words are impossible, a heavenly command inspires us to rest our lips on the skin of those in misfortune and save them with the warmth of our vitality. When the angel had disappeared someone else came up, again with a kiss.

For Judas it wasn't enough to point Jesus out with his finger, or indicate who he was by his face or the colour of his tunic – the night was dark as pitch and all the shadows looked alike. So, in order to avoid any mistake, a precise distinguishing act was needed, and from very near. He had to kiss him. Once he'd made his way right up to the Master, perhaps Judas felt he couldn't justify his unreasonable and awkward proximity unless he carried it through with a kiss. Or perhaps he could have withheld the brotherly gesture, but at the last moment the wretched man became two people again and with dizzy courage leapt out of his treachery – like a captured fish leaping back into the water from a boat – and wanted to savour the Lord's cheek? Was he perhaps desperately sincere and happy for the brief moment that a kiss lasts? Did his kiss placate his envy of John whose head had been resting on Jesus' breast a few hours before? For the last time the Master's fair beard was subject to his senses, and his sweet calm breath seemed to blow away the horror of what he, Judas, was accomplishing, seemed to bring him back once more into the committee of thirteen, to wake him up from the bad dream . . .

Perhaps there passed from Judas's lips to Christ's ear some word that remained unheard by the evangelist and didn't even cause a tremor in the freezing air of the garden. And was it perhaps because of this word that Jesus called him 'friend'? All this is open to conjecture; and it wouldn't have been more than a momentary impulse – for a little earlier the traitor had said words of calculated conspiracy to the crowd armed with swords and sticks; he'd said: *'The one I kiss will be him: seize him and take him away under a good guard.'* The contact of that mouth was in very truth the beginning of his bodily passion; it was the first act of physical brutality, the first wound.

NINEPINS

. . . so going forward he said to them: 'Who are you looking for?' They shouted: 'Jesus of Nazareth.' 'I'm Jesus of Nazareth', he told them, and as soon as he said this they backed away and fell to the ground.

These men were soon going to lay him low with acts of brutality and violence. In a few moments Christ would hand himself over to them, let himself be bound and do nothing to avert their blows. But in this first round he decided to reverse the roles; he would be the harmless, almost comic, executioner and they would be the victims. For the passion to be prevented there was no need for the twelve legions of angels whom the Father – as he was soon to say to Peter – could send down to rout his enemies; his voice was enough ('That's me'), and the rabble fell down like ninepins. His voice had quietened a storm and raised Lazarus from the dead.

Leave them there among the rocks, all piled up and ridiculous under your spell, petrified with a wild fear that they're about to kill the Son of man. Leave them there, Lord, and let's go home. *'But all this is happening so that the scriptures and prophets may be fulfilled.'* And in the scriptures it was indicated that those idiotic puppets should get up again (so there they were getting up again and dusting their clothes) and that their fear should evaporate; that Jesus, whose immediate concern was about the fate of his followers, should say: *'So if you're looking for me, let these others go off.'* He had chastised them with the sobriety and indulgence of an aristocrat. Now he freed them from their flattened paralysis and gave them back their dull-witted murderers' freedom. But before putting himself into their clutches, he lashed them with a final, peaceful rebuke: *'You've come armed with swords and sticks to seize me as though I were a thief. I was sitting among you every day, teaching in the temple, and you never arrested me.'*

Sticks and swords . . . what martial courage! First the push-over, then the irony. After that it would be humility, patience and silence. Caiaphas, Pilate. The spit, the blows, the curses of the people. Until the nails in the hands and feet.

THE SWORD AND THE CARESS

One of them struck the High Priest's servant and cut off his right ear. But Jesus said: 'Stop. That's enough.' And he touched the man's ear and cured it.

That was the last miracle. I don't know how much blood there is when an ear's cut off. Perhaps a cupful, perhaps a basinful. In this case there were only a few drops because the miracle took place at once; the ear was soldered to the head without a scar – just with a fiat.

We can be sure that the blood splashing on to the grass that night in Gethsemane was a prelude to the grand theme of the blood to be shed in a full red stream with the scourging, the nails, the thorns and the spear: the theme of the lamb slaughtered for all of us. But on this particular page we find the first intimation of it all. No mention is made in the miracles or exploits of any blood visibly spurting out. Malchus is the only blood-stained protagonist. It was the destiny of that obscure scullion, brought in to carry an extra torch, to mix his blood on the garden turf with the mystical blood of the Covenant.

And Simon Peter, who had a sword . . . Had Peter a sword? The gospel gives away no secrets. It suddenly and without preamble reveals surprising and unexpected truths. What was that sword doing among the twelve? Who'd got hold of it, and how? Possibly they'd kept it hidden from him and he'd always pretended he didn't know about it, because even that sword – that comic sword whose career was confined to cutting off an ear – was enumerated in the arsenal of objects in the gospel, in the inventory preserved by the Father in the abstruse labyrinths of eternity. It had to play its part in enabling him to pronounce yet another word of mercy.

So the last phrase he left with his followers – even after those at the cenacle with all their solemnity of a farewell without postscript – was a firm and loving reproach: '*Put the sword back into its scabbard.*' The last gesture they were to remember – before the bloody and already other-worldly glimmers of the passion carried him away – was of this man stooping to the ground to pick up an amputated ear and rejoin it to a cheek with a caress.

Whenever in history I come across the crusades, or Christian armies, or even an odd cutting word addressed by us to others, I suddenly see again the Master stooping to retrieve an ear; and his wordless caress to the beloved enemy among the threatening torches.

THE CHEEK

One of the guards struck him and said: 'Is that the way you answer the High Priest?'

It was in the hall of the Sanhedrin that Christ received his first blow. He had been on earth for thirty-three years and no hard object had fallen on him, nothing corporal had ever struck him. In the homely silence of Nazareth, with Mary and Joseph, he'd never heard the echo of a blow even on the household animals, nor on the gentle donkey that carried them to Egypt. Until that moment Jesus had preserved a second sort of virginity – of someone who had never been hit, of a skin bearing no mark of violence.

The soldier's hand fell on his cheek. Like frightened doves, Mary's caresses flew away from that cheek, away from the courtyard of the Sanhedrin and no one knows where they found refuge. There remained the bitter stinging of the blood. Which was wars, massacres, the killers and the killed. Written on his cheek was the history of the world.

TWO TURBANS

... first they led him to Annas ... and Annas sent him bound to Caiaphas who was High Priest that year.

By now all was prearranged for his death. Caiaphas had made it quite clear: '*It's fitting that one man should die for the people.*'

Annas, Caiaphas ... Who were they? Why did they want this gentle man to die? Why did they stay up in their palaces that night among the comings and goings of the torches?

Those two men bore the largest responsibility for Jesus' death, which was the most scandalous and iniquitous of all deaths; their pertinacity was the most implacable. Beneath those two turbans – that of the old, all-powerful father-in-law and that of the younger son-in-law who then held office as High Priest – the plot was set going that would remove the prophet, overthrow at great risk the popularity he enjoyed among the people, and force their will on their Roman master who would ask to wash his hands of the affair. Christ's crucifixion, as stark and remorseless as a theorem, had already taken place beneath those two turbans – from the first lash of the scourge down to the thrust of the spear. Those two men lacked Judas's rash emotionalism and heedless ignorance as well as Pilate's short-sighted apathy. '*He's guilty of death*', shouted Caiaphas, and ended the encounter with his prisoner by the theatrical gesture of tearing his robes.

What had offended them so much? Or what was there about this vagabond, this street witch-doctor, that frightened them? The vagabond and witch-doctor hadn't been content – unfortunately for him! – with curing the blind and the lame and raising one or two people from the dead. He'd also been talking, and talking too much. '*The time has come*', he said to the woman at the well, '*when you won't worship the Father either on this mountain or in Jerusalem ... God is spirit and those who worship him should worship him in spirit and in truth.*' And in public: '*Don't let yourselves be called masters, because you only have one master and you're*

175

all brothers.' And again: *'It's a bad look out for you hypocrites, you scribes and Pharisees; you're like whitened sepulchres, splendid outside but full of dead bones and filth within.'*

What was there left of a high priest's job if the temple of Jerusalem could be replaced by a fig-tree on a hill or a moth-eaten stool in a hayloft as a place for adoring the free God? And if no one could be called master? And if the purest caste of Hebrews could be vilified in insulting language, what would become of the rabbis, of Caiaphas, Annas, and their turbans?

With sadistic spite the outraged Caiaphas interrogated the man standing before him with ropes round his wrists, the man who by Caiaphas's firm decision had only a few hours to live. But Jesus didn't want to waste the short twilight of his life repeating a doctrine that wasn't drawn up in paragraphs or philosophical treatises but, if it was living, henceforward lay inside those who had taken it back home – and in everlasting destiny. *'Why are you asking me questions? Ask those who heard what I was talking about. They know perfectly well what I said.'*

And to the hysterical uproar of the corrupt witnesses who calumniated him and contradicted each other, to the pressures of the judge (*'Haven't you anything to answer about what those witnesses say against you?'*), and to all the sinister brain-washing thrust on him that night in the palace, *Jesus remained silent and answered nothing.*

Yet what made his death certain wasn't this particular silence. It wasn't anger at Jesus' invective on the part of dethroned Caiaphas and the other synagogue bureaucrats that sent him to the place of execution. It was when Christ serenely opened his mouth to answer the fiery, raging question we all keep on asking him:

'I call on you to tell us whether you're the Christ, the Son of God.'

'I am', he answered.

It was then that, amid the hiss of his torn robes, a stronger and more revengeful passion took possession of Caiaphas. It's called superstition. We can minister to God and serve him in our own way, but we have a horror of meeting him. If he comes too near, we have only one way of defending ourselves from him, Caiaphas's way. By killing him. Killing him even in the name of God, hiding ourselves behind a misty idol, shouting at him that it's a blasphemy to appear alive in our midst. *'He's blasphemed. What further witnesses do we need?'* It was superstition that killed the Son of God.

BEHIND THE BANDAGE

Then the men holding Jesus made fun of him and struck him. And some of them bandaged his eyes and spat in his face and hit him, saying: 'Now, Christ, guess who hit you that time.'

Besides Christ's great daytime passion there was also this minor nocturnal passion that only lasted a few minutes, the brief orgy enjoyed by the faceless cowards who cuffed him in the semi-darkness of the flares.

Christ scourged at the pillar, Christ struggling up the hill, and then at last Christ in splendour on the cross; on those occasions he rose to a level of solemn and adorable beauty; at those stages, if merely with the plasticity of his agonized body, he *demonstrated* that he wasn't just a man but a superhuman symbol. But at the point we're describing, when he was blinded by a bandage, with the spit of the rabble dribbling down his beard, bullied like a donkey that doesn't want to budge, amid the shouts and laughter of those drunken torturers – what about that? . . . At this point, if he wants me to recognize him as the one who has come down from eternity to make me eternal, he is asking me for an improbable faith. Why such an ordeal of abjection and ridicule? What was going on behind the bandage? What would his eyes have told me had I taken off the strip covering them? Would they have freed me for ever from my unbelief, because the loftiest moment of the passion was then taking place? And did his eyes hold, in that moment, the light of all the mysteries, the distances of the stars in the cosmos and the serene explanation of why all this machinery for pain – the universe – was once created?

THE SLEEPWALKER

And he went out from the place and wept bitterly.

During the night in which Christ began dying, this bitter weeping broke out and re-echoed from one end of the story to the other. The first blood was spilt in the garden, the first blow was delivered by a servant in the palace, and the first sob arose beside a brushwood fire – because *the servants and the guards lit a fire in the middle of the courtyard; it was cold, and they sat around it to warm themselves.*

A man wept because a cock crowed. Peter's cock hailed no dawn, for it was the depth of night and dawn still lay ahead. Invisible in the backyards of Jerusalem, that fowl was obedient to the plot of the master who had given it a secret mission, and punctually started to crow so as to wake a sleepwalker. It had to crow twice and at its second crow the sleepwalker pulled himself together: like those unhappy people who wander about at night, he was suddenly awakened and looked around in a daze, the sob surging in his throat like blood from a vein. The group around the fire stared at him. What a grotesque transformation! Until a few moments ago this man had been arrogantly and aggressively loquacious and doing everything to make plain that he was one of them. Caiaphas's portress, then the maid, then that third person, and yet another, had tried in vain to make him admit the opposite . . . *'Woman, I don't know him. I don't understand what you're talking about . . .'* '*My friend, I don't know what you mean . . .*' Then he swore in order to put an end to it: '*I don't know that man.*' His voice was so loud that he couldn't hear the first cock-crow. All he could feel was a kind of bitterness or irritation against himself and his past – at leaving his peaceful fisherman's nets so as to get involved in such an unpleasant adventure; and, yes, against that vagabond who'd dragged him into such an awful mess. Above all he could feel, between his heart and his stomach, that icy octopus we call fear, and he was trying without success to crush it by

178

his rough and cordial talkativeness. Why on earth had he gone and got himself stuck in that courtyard in the wake of that other person who'd already been done in for certain? Heaven knew what they were up to inside there or what they'd do to *him*, Peter. He would have liked to change his nose and beard because they went on saying they recognized him; he would have liked to get rid of his heavy Galilean accent because they said, damn it, *'You're recognizable by your accent, too'*. And as he couldn't evaporate in that group of people, he looked at them with smarmy love, and threw an odd piece of wood on the fire. Wasn't that communal fire enough to make a bit of comradeship spring up between them, so that they'd leave him in peace? Evidently not, because now another wretched person came up: *'But surely I saw you in the garden with him?'* Then he began swearing. 'I don't know him, I don't know him, I don't know him . . .'

Into the silence following Peter's rage the second cock-crow cut sharp and clear. Peter heard it. And following that bird's hoarse cry there came once more – but he alone heard it – a certain voice, a certain phrase: *'I'll tell you the truth: today, in fact this very night, before the cock crows twice you'll deny me three times.'* Where had he heard it? At supper. Who had said it? He had, the man who was coming out of the door, who turned and looked at him, just gave him a look and left his gaze behind him when, with back turned, he went off with the guards.

Christ went off and left him one last gift: bitter-sweet tears, the intoxication of shame and repentance, that blessed abyss of childhood we call crying – which doesn't make us pure but for a few divine moments makes us sincere and full of memories and hopes, which liberates us from all actuality except what is beneficently making us weep. Peter wept over his past life as a man, over his early faults as a boy, down to this ultimate disgrace. He wept, too, though without knowing it, over his sins that would continue for thousands of years, over the denials, mistakes and acts of cowardice of the men who – according to Christ's command – would succeed him. For them no cock would crow to make them pull themselves together.

We are all sleepwalkers. Does this mean that all of us, like

Peter in that courtyard, are unconsciously talking and acting like sleepwalkers? Until a cock wakes us up and makes us pass all our tomorrows in tears.

PONTIUS PILATE'S DIARY
FOR POSTERITY

'Don't get mixed up with that just man, because today in a dream I had to suffer a lot on his account.'

Since my wife started having those dreams I've decided to keep a diary. Or better, I'll call it a 'letter to posterity': so as to explain myself (or justify myself, or rehabilitate myself?) to those who come after me. For among other things that Claudia told me last night in bed after her dream, she said that people will talk about me for thousands of years (I wouldn't like to believe this, and in any case I don't), and she's in agony lest they'll talk about me as a symbol of shame. In any case to keep a record or a document or whatever you like to call it is part of the *officia,* of what is right and fitting for someone with my job, that of a bureaucrat. The truth is (I say this rather for myself than for those yet to be born who may read this) that I wasn't born a bureaucrat. I had good teachers: I was a lively boy – so they told me (and women too . . .) – a boy of talent and character. My strong suit was philosophy, or perhaps drama: fine dialogue, well-balanced phrases full of meaning yet without rhetoric (I wrote a couple of plays when I was young, stuff I lost in a shipwreck a few years ago). My idol certainly isn't Caesar, but rather Lucretius and, even more, Democritus and Epicurus . . . I wasn't born a bureaucrat, but that's what I have become: it's a *forma mentis* that stiffens your sinews like rheumatism.

I was talking about my wife, and her reasons – or rather her insinuations – which made me decide as from today to set down on paper my dealings with Jesus of Nazareth. Claudia dreamt fantastic things about that young man (and goes on insisting they're true even when she's awake). She dreamt that after his death he'll rise again, no less, and dominate the world until the end of time – after Rome has fallen to dust. Delusions? Who knows? It's my conviction (don't laugh, it's true and I'm very much of a *vir uxorius*) that my wife has a gift of second sight, even of prophecy. I've experienced it more than once. And the fact is that for some hours I've been fighting for that man whom those bats of Jews want to kill at all costs – the gods alone know why. I keep asking myself why I'm doing this. I'm a Roman: not particularly inclined to bloodshed but not over emotional or gentle either. Rome has accustomed me to seeing in the amphitheatre – though without particularly enjoying it, let me say – barbarians being quartered and torn to bits. What value has a life for me, particularly his life? You'll say it's Claudia's predictions, her sinister and warning dreams, and her obvious partiality for him. But that's not all. The fact is the man has something ... Yes, let's say it openly (with the concrete courage customary among us Romans and with a philosopher's lack of prejudice): I was not a little impressed by him.

Those horrible barbarians brought him to me very early this morning and asked me to put him on trial (and the mornings are so fragrant just now; the languor and scents of spring made me want to pass my time declaiming Catullus or even Ovid ...). They say that Christ is a subversive element, he stops tribute being paid to Caesar and claims to be a king. I questioned him (he's good-looking and looks at me firmly and gently; an unusual man). About the matter of being a king, he answered that he is a king but his kingdom isn't here below. Bah. If he's a dreamer or a mystic there's no understanding why he has that gang around him and frequents public places and mixes with common people. Above all it's beyond comprehension why he upsets his own national hierarchy so much. But he was quite clear about being a king. He also said: '*That's why I was born and came into the world, to be a witness to the truth*', and he went on: '*Anyone on the side of truth listens to my voice.*'

I must confess that at this point in the interrogation I would have been very ready for a discussion with him. Truth! An abstract, universal concept: philosophy. It doesn't happen every day in this country with its bastardized superstitions that you have a dialogue with anyone about culture and thought.

THE PASSION

It's a long time since I've heard a couple of quick rejoinders on the conceptual level ... Let's be clear about it: I don't believe that truth exists; I'm on the side of the sceptics. I don't even want to know what truth is. As a result of my studies I know too much to believe in such simple ideas as that. But I rose to the bait deliberately. I asked him, with that ring in my voice and with those pauses that have enabled me to make a career for myself, half-ironical, half-questing: '*What is truth?*'

But there wasn't time for a debate about truth. Those Jewish monkeys were pressing round the doors of the praetorium. When I discovered that he was a Galilean, and hence within Herod's jurisdiction, I decided that Herod must sort things out. Herod happens to be in Jerusalem today. That vacuous pumpkin was delighted to agree because he hoped to see him perform a miracle. He's a complete imbecile. And he was doubly disappointed. First because Jesus performed no miracle, and second because he wouldn't answer a single word to any of Herod's questions. That, I must admit, made me feel even warmer towards the young Jew. As for Herod, he thought the talented young man must be mad, and he couldn't think of anything more witty to do than send him back to me dressed in the white tunic they use for lunatics. The real lunatic is Herod. But now, *pro forma*, the tetrarch and I have become firm friends again.

As soon as he came back into my net (and to tell the truth I hoped he'd slipped out of it) I took a stricter line in his defence against those synagogue camels, and tried to use traps and ruses to save him and nail them: '*I haven't found in him one single fault you've accused him of,*' I told them petulantly, '*nothing that deserves death. So I'll have him scourged and then release him.*' This may seem a fine example of coherent Roman justice: you say he's innocent and you have him scourged. But I had my plan. It's a nasty business administering justice in a country where there's nothing but fanaticism, hypocrisy and pride. There's no governing these people without compromises and no holding a proper trial. They want murder and bloodshed. When they see him hurt and all swollen and reduced by our champion floggers to a point worse than death, then their

182

bloodthirsty lust will be appeased. They'll go home satisfied and Christ will escape with his skin. At the age of thirty you get over this type of scar in a few weeks.

Then I thought of another plan. They have a custom whereby I have to free a condemned man every Passover. And it so happens that, here in jail, I've just the right fodder for the scaffold, a fellow called Barabbas – a turbulent murderer and a danger to everyone's life. I felt sure that in the bargaining Christ would win, so I turned to the people and said: '*Which of the two do you want me to set free for you? Barabbas or Jesus called the Christ?*' I felt sure, and I stress the point, that I would checkmate those turbaned bats. You only have to look at Barabbas to feel afraid. But who could have believed it? They all shouted together: '*Barabbas! Not him, but Barabbas. Take that man out of the world and give us Barabbas.*'

Then I played my last card, the one I've told you about. I had him flogged and smashed up by blows and lashes; because if *I* wasn't capable of defending him, his appearance when they saw him again would surely be defence enough.

A BRILLIANT PLAN

So Pilate took Jesus and had him scourged.

Cheer up, Jesus, Pilate's plan is a brilliant one. The lashes inflicted on you will be appalling but they'll save your life. The morsels of flesh sticking to the whips will transform you into such a pitiful monster that your passion will be over with that hail of blows. Pilate's right: at thirty you recover from that in a few weeks, and even that crown of thorns that they're pressing down on your head (very long, robust thorns, but hard enough to go in where the soldiers are hammering them, because your skull is made of bone and is resistant) – that crown won't kill you either. The cloak they've put around you and the reed they've stuck in your hand as a sceptre – all that's a providential piece of theatre. Disguised in this way as a king, the equivocation that has so enraged them will be eliminated –

namely, that you're claiming a kingdom, in this or another world. Your crushed and grotesque caricature will put paid to the drama. With the insults of those men who beat you and spit on you, who hammer at your head and mock you – kneeling down and calling you king of the Jews – we'll see the anger of a whole people suddenly evaporate, as with a bloodletting.

You're in the red-hot furnace of agony, blows are falling not on you any more but on your second, flayed, body; on your crimsoned sinews and nerves where the slightest touch causes a spasm – that's where the leather of the whip falls. You haven't made a sound, but if you could howl your cry would break our eardrums.

But we have faith in Pilate; and also in men, in their pity or at least in their disgust.

ECCE HOMO

And Jesus came out wearing the crown of thorns and the purple cloak.

Pilate the playwright, the strategist of human psychology, the pupil of Lucretius, was putting on his masterpiece. Here he was on the balcony of the praetorium with Christ at his side, and in a phrase of studied understatement he indicated him with: *'Here's the man.'*

At the same time he gave Christ a sideways glance and felt satisfied: that eye like a purple sponge, that mask of blood, that blow that had opened his forehead – surely these were just what was needed ...

It was a moment of suspense. All the houses of the city would fall on one another, the landscape and architecture would crumble with horror into new shapes, and in the flattened expanse there would be no more Jerusalem with its hills and temples, but just chunks of quartz of all different shapes and sizes, and saurians of race unknown would cringe and quench their thirst in lunar craters under a livid sky. Because the man had appeared; the man as he was, and not merely that Jew on trial; and the man was thus: a scarecrow harrowed by the fury

184

of evil, torn to pieces by a hatred without logic or responsibility – alike reproach and victim. The man who was one great vertical wound, which mothers would wash to no avail, a bloody discharge dressed in a red rag, because they said he was king of this world.

CONTINUATION OF PILATE'S DIARY

More incredible still: no sooner had I produced him on the balcony than their leaders, the guards and all the rabble behind them began demanding that I should have him killed. *'I don't find any guilt in him'*, I cried, and that was the fourth, the fifth or the tenth time on this tedious Friday that I threw the same refrain back into their faces: *'What harm has he done?'* As a Roman who has studied and venerated our law for years, nothing irritates me more than unjust actions, than fanaticism which tries to reverse the cold but wonderful decisions of justice. I was in a fury against their pig-headed barbarism, and so I began venting my rage in a thousand different ways to set him free (o how I would have loved to have ordered a charge of legionaries with drawn swords to fall on that rabble!). I went down to the forecourt and sat in my chair of office so as to pass judgment on that poor fellow with due solemnity. But the crowd went on shouting – you should have heard the brutes: *'We have a law, and according to that law the man should die because he made himself the Son of God.'* *'If you set him free you're no friend of Caesar's; anyone who turns himself into a king is against Caesar.'* And I, who have a strong voice too, tried to shout them down, going so far as to flatter their patriotic ambitions: *'Here's your king.'* But they said, *'Away with him! Crucify him! Crucify him!'* *'Shall I crucify your king?'* I then asked, and those ruffians replied: *'We have no king but Caesar.'* I blocked my ears and went back to the palace. I tried to have a talk with Claudia who wept and embraced me, but we couldn't hear each other speak because of the bestial din that came from the square outside and shook the foundations of my palace.

RED THROATS

But they shouted . . .

'Crucify him! Crucify him!' Everyone was shouting it, and those with strong voices gazed into the open mouths of the others and challenged them and tried to humiliate them with the roar of their more powerful lungs. Excited women bawled in shriller tones, while children, lifted up in their mothers' arms, repeated the cry (but mispronounced it – what did the long word mean?): 'Crucify him! Crucify him!'

If they went on shouting as loud as this, shouting those two words and those two terrible words only, they'd crush the Roman governor and put to flight the mighty legions encamped in Judea who would be terrified by their mob courage about killing God.

The rabble had only one weapon for escaping from slavery – slavery to Caesar and the harsher slavery to God – and this was their red throats. Once they saw him hanging from the cross that evening, their homeland and their hearts and their women and their herds would at last be their own, would belong to each and every one of them. They'd had enough of masters. They'd had enough of magicians who lulled storms and raised the dead: they wanted nature as she is, predictable in the course of her laws and with no blackmail about eternal life. 'Crucify him!'

All were shouting it. And in the intoxication of their howling they became like the children they held in their arms, they ceased to know what that word 'crucify' meant. It was some dark song of their forefathers, some dusky imploration, an unbridled horse galloping out into the night and all that could now be done was to cling to its mane, shut your eyes, and shout.

A man who didn't take part in the communal cry was wandering through the crowd beneath the praetorium. A little while ago they'd carried him in triumph, offered him drinks and

186

said, 'Go home and enjoy yourself'. But he'd stayed around. He'd seen the bloodstained man on the balcony – his defeated rival – and was now staring at those open mouths that were nailing him to the cross. He didn't go home. He'd have liked to go back to prison. He was a murderer – called Barabbas.

PILATE'S DIARY: CONCLUSION

To conclude. I've had one last encounter with the accused – a very short one. While those people outside were shouting that Jesus says he's the Son of God, I went back and asked him where he came from, in a word what were his origins. He didn't answer; not even when I reminded him that his life was in my hands. Then he told me that I'd have no power over him if it hadn't been given me from on high, and that was why those who had handed him over to me were much guiltier than me. A circle of concepts I didn't understand very clearly, except to deduce that he sees me as a party to the guilt, if to a lesser degree.

I don't know what responsibility or wrong could be found in me for what I've done throughout this episode. And to confirm once and for all my lack of co-responsibility, I went out to those crows and said: *'I'm innocent of the blood of this just man: it's up to you.'* And I ordered a bowl of water to be brought and dipped my hands in it in front of them to show that I wanted to cleanse myself of any responsibility. To show *them*. But I've written this short record because I want to wash my hands of Jesus Christ also and above all in front of *you*, people yet to be born. The only answer I got from those lunatics was a shout: *'His blood be on us and on our children.'*

So now, what will be will be. Permit me to conclude with a personal footnote, though it may not matter a fig to you. Perhaps my wife was right: she's good but I believe she's a magician. My feelings for her are a mixture of devotion and fear. When they brought me the news that Christ had risen from the tomb I felt a superstition of which I ought to be ashamed, and said to myself: Perhaps the curtain hasn't yet fallen on this drama. The fact is that since then my life has been divided between two Pilates: the Pilate who is ever increasingly sceptical and wants to grow old in a library between his Epicurus and his Lucretius, and the Pilate who carries the horror within him that what his wife dreamt was true and that consequently I've collaborated in ... And then there's the dizzy abyss of suicide. But I haven't the courage to take my life. I don't believe even in death, not even in nothingness.

Somebody said (so did Claudia) that there might be a third way: that of devoting myself to his teaching (if teaching it is); in a word, of joining up with his followers and even having myself crucified ... at least it would suit me better than the way things are now. But it's too late. I'm fifty. I don't expect inner conversions and I no longer expect good news. Except the news that Rome will soon recall me and put me on the retiring list.

INSECTS

Jesus set out carrying his cross . . .

Now he had to get going. Now he had to move his feet with the conviction that this wasn't any cross but his-own-cross, just as that crippled boy is my son and that old woman with cancer is my mother; it wasn't a piece of wood but a piece of our body, and our body isn't just flesh and bone but also our destiny.

Now the debate with men was over, and the interplay of cowardice and betrayal and denial and ruses to save him or bargain for him or lose him – all was finished, over and done with. We are now in the open air, the sky is wide, and lean goats are blocking the way or, untethered, watching from the ravines. Judas, Caiaphas, Peter and Pilate are now in the past, dead or desperate or having a peaceful day moving towards supper and bed; dwarfs and nonentities have cleared the stage for the protagonist's action.

The protagonist was that human insect climbing up and up, like insects we see in the furrows of the earth obstinately dragging along an enormous crumb or a dead grub; and could we look at things from a great height even Christ there beneath us might look as though he loved his booty and was dragging it towards some jealous ant-heap.

Whereas he was moving towards the black abyss of the end. And meanwhile everything was getting shorter, drawing to a close, every step was a scissor-snip in the fabric of longings and regrets, cutting off the last vain hopes of being saved. How remote and absurd his fear in the garden now seemed! What was near was this dull kindness of things, of the objects that marked his path and slipped away behind him under his tread: stones, roots, bedstraw, sheep's dung. The things children notice when they wander through the country, that we don't see later in life, though now Christ saw them once more and they gave him a small, ecstatic moment of repose, an instant of playful thoughtlessness. Now he would let his cross fall and follow with his eye that mole delaying outside its hole; he would pick out that sparkling stone scaled with mica. It was towards this that he was going – like every man knowingly about to die – towards earliest infancy, this treasure lost and betrayed along the hypocritical march of the years. This was why he felt no more fear, for he had no more thoughts, but only his memories and fantasies.

Soon it would all be over. Soon there would be no more bellowing soldiers or women weeping for him, but moles and sparkling stones and that yellow butterfly that had alighted on the cross without making it heavier and was now flying in front of him.

Jesus' spirit lay within that dream of small creatures, but his body lay under a bestial fatigue, his back and shoulders and feet were in an adult's hell. That was why, as he carried the cross, he paused, reeled, and crashed to the ground. And he wasn't to be moved either by the men's curses or his own will to get up. Christ was broken. Someone had to help him or take his place to the top of Calvary.

THE ORCHESTRA

A large crowd of women followed him beating their breasts and lamenting over him.

On that day all the women of Jerusalem were mothers. Mothers never go away, never give up, and aren't afraid of soldiers. They knew that a son's passion has to be accompanied by notes of weeping and wailing; they knew that when a man dies he needs music, that it's their task to play his farewell to life, and that this had been so for thousands of years. So the women-mothers, those instruments of pain, put together their poor orchestra behind the cross: that little old woman who was shouting was the clarinet, the fat widow was the oboe, the girl was the harp, and that other one who was supporting her was the lute.

These people brought an element of tenderness to Calvary. On and on they went, until the condemned man's last death-rattle, without either collapsing or feeling macabre horror. Could they have done so, they would have licked the body, they would have cleansed it of every scab and every insect, because for a mother there's no transition between the living and the dead, her first care is tenderness and it's also her last, and the son is kept clean and spotless as long as people can see him.

The son. Because this man wasn't the Messiah any more, he was their communal child. They refused to be redeemed daughters, that cross didn't concern them, they were ready to barter their eternal life for one more breath of his agony.

But Christ was against them, and it was only to them that he spoke at this last stage of his pilgrimage: '. . . *don't cry about me but about yourselves and your children, because the day will come when it will be said, "Blessed are the sterile, and the wombs that haven't conceived, and the breasts that haven't given milk".'*

So he had shaken himself out of his childlike stupor that had consoled him in that sparkle of stones and butterflies; and it was to confront these women and challenge their blind and pagan passion as mammals: *'Then people will begin to say to the mountains, "fall on us", and to the hills, "cover us up".'*

But the mothers didn't listen, they closed their ears to his warnings, they didn't hear his blasphemy. For them sons had to go on being born, their breasts were rounder than those hills and invulnerable to all maledictions. This ninth beatitude of sterility that Christ added to those he had one day sung on the Mount didn't affect them; they knew by experience that there's no greater blessedness than to feel one's own milk being sucked.

'Because if it goes like this with the green wood, what will happen to the dry?' Christ added, thereby raising black veils from their faces. The mothers answered wildly that children should flourish on the earth whether the wood that went on the fire was green or dry; for no one would ever be able to crucify their memories. And when that hour sounded, each became the sum of her cradle memories, recalling how she had washed Christ in the kitchen tub and carried him into the garden to see the bees.

No, those words didn't even brush against the Jerusalem mothers, and the person who said them was out of his senses and had forgotten that he had been their baby.

'Then people will begin to say to the mountains, "fall on us", and to the hills, "cover us up".'

But the orchestra didn't stop, it drowned the threatening voice of the crucified man. For them the day when the hills would fall on their heads was this very day; the end of the world wasn't some apocalyptic tomorrow, and they felt no fear of it. It was enough that he should leave to one of them the face of the dead son on a handkerchief (as legend has it). And all would be mothers still, and for ever.

THE BLIND OX

As they were going out they fell on a man . . .

Who was this dark man with a red furrow on his shoulder?

191

He was someone coming from the opposite direction to that of the procession. Everything about him was *opposite*, from the colour of his skin to the colour of his thoughts which *knew* nothing and didn't want to imagine anything. Simon of Cyrene knew nothing about prophecies concerning a Messiah and Redeemer. He was altogether extraneous in this Jewish affair and story of a kingdom. His only kingdom, not much bigger than a table-cloth, was his farm. He was now returning from there, and from the fields where evening had brought the first cool breath to the turf and to him. And he was different from his fields, he was a man, only because at this time of day he didn't stay out under the moon with the stooked-up corn but was making this long trek back to a house. The evening lay heavy on him, though not with poetic fragrance; and also a huge weariness; and also a desire to push open the door, sit down to a steaming bowl of soup and, during his silent supper, savour the smell of his children and his bed, his only possession and dull reward for a day just like every other day.

But no, it wasn't quite like every other day. For this evening fate singled out him, just him, the black peasant, from among the countless millions of men called to walk the earth from Adam to the last day. He was all that was most anonymous at a most anonymous time, and then Mystery forced him for a short while to be Christ's opposite number.

So Simon was still working, just when he'd hoped the day was over. What's more he was giving his labour without payment. As usual, he said nothing, but growled under the weight of the cross. And yet in spite of himself there lay a conspiracy of charity, if not in his Cyrenean heart, at least in his body bent into a caryatid, and in his neck streaming with sweat.

He arrived at the top. He wiped his hands on his labourer's overalls and went off without a glance behind him, quickening his pace as he got away and then finally breaking into a run. In his bed to which he hurried for refuge – skipping supper – his shoulder hurt him. As from tomorrow he'd go home a different way, he'd go the long way round.

Simon of Cyrene, perhaps you're the loneliest and worst-treated brother in the whole gospel. For Christ's companions and the Palestine crowds there were parables, miracles, beatitudes, and long and enchanting periods of training. For you there was only brute ignorance, the blindness of an ox ploughing the earth of Calvary with the tail of the cross. When you got home you were still frightened and your fear didn't fade even when you went to sleep, and you had a throbbing shoulder. Yet you had a sublime privilege: the opposite of John's privilege who rested his head on Christ's shoulder, whereas on your shoulder . . .

When your time was up, Simon, how did you die? You didn't know, you never knew. On your deathbed you invoked your African idols and the god Baal; or you implored Rufus and Alexander – those sons of yours the evangelist mysteriously knew by name – to turn your pillow. But you entered straight into the Kingdom without baptism or prayer. Your hands were empty, but that scar on your shoulder showed you had released Christ from many ounces of pain.

You handled the supreme relic whose bits and pieces have been scattered heaven knows where throughout the world – one bit would make us happy for ever – and you did so without emotion, without blessing it, and with rough, rancorous hands. Yet the cross made you suffer. So come on then, you first unwilling martyr.

THE THIRD HOUR

And he was crucified at the third hour.

For two thousand years that third hour has stood still on the hour-glass of time.

For two thousand years we've had that third hour under our eyes and under our fingers: depicted on canvas, silver, wood, mother-of-pearl. From the day of our birth that triangle of the crucifix has been in our daily senses like the moon or a flag or a spoon or a wheel; it lives in everyone's domestic baggage. When we die someone we can't see through the haze will put it to our lips. That cold polished shape is the last thing to which we dedicate our love.

Almost always he stands for tranquillity and familiarity – now. He's the ancient and naked little man hanging at the bottom of a rosary; or along the Tyrolese byways beneath a thick roof of fir-trees and discoloured by rain, where we salute him with a sigh as we turn to enjoy the delights of the countryside.

Sometimes the more bizarre artificers have given him movement, have twisted him around as though they wanted to tear him away from the wood and make him dance. But the nails always hold him down at the three points in hands and feet, so that he can't be made into something else, or freed to form an unfamiliar image. It's always a triangle. And now it's difficult to be moved by that triangle even if an artist gives his Jesus a contorted mouth and a rolling eye, or if a rough craftsman makes realistic drops of blood flow from the nails with red lead. 'Come and look at this,' the antique-dealer says, 'how d'you like this one? The Venus costs more, but this ivory Christ is beautiful in its way, especially on a velvet background.'

He has become an object. We've sought to mineralize him, we make him pathetic or precious, we turn him into gold or a morsel of bread, so as to free ourselves from his agony and death as a man. The more we reproduce him the more we forget him and his third hour which sounded millions of hours ago on the hill with real grass, real blood and real minutes.

The little mineral man was crucified that day and he was as tall as me and there was nothing to him but fear and flesh. Since then craftsmen have laboriously with their tools pierced the material – whether marble, bronze or whatever – of the finely sculpted hands. But at the third hour the craftsmen on Calvary carved that crucified man with no trouble at all. No art was needed to bang in the nails with hammers, nor any red lead to make a furrow of blood from the hands and feet of the statue; the mouth and eyes were wonderfully twisted merely by hoisting him up with a jolt on the cross and leaving him there to be attacked by tetanus.

Up there, after that first jolt, we no longer grasp the slow unravelling of his tissues, the spread of gangrene, and his raging thirst. Christ seems tranquil. His quiet composure makes us think that his whole existence was like that – in the shape of a cross-bow with his arms halfway between salutation and resignation; that his figure upraised in the air is the definitive figure of a man when, from being a squalid larva, he turns into a dragonfly.

The world went back to the peace it needed. He tried to turn it into a great cathedral organ, he had dug music from herds of pigs, dry bread, whores and the dead; but the world preferred to return to the silence of its hills, the smoke of its villages worm-eaten with lechery and boredom. Nain, Jericho, Capernaum and Bethany, you put two nails in his hands to silence his music.

I would like to be a saint at least for a moment, because I was taught that saints fall into ecstasy before this ancient triangle. Saints and the dying. Drawing his last breath, the little man freed himself from his ice, shattered the silver, and confided the mystery of the third hour.

THOSE FEW WORDS

And Jesus said: 'Father, forgive them . . .'

Up there he couldn't move his hands. But he could still speak. Not to these men, they didn't listen to him any more, all they could do was to shout their final taunts. But to the Father. He could still do not *something* for these men, but *the thing*. He could save them from punishment. Shelter them from the hurricane with his dying shoulders: *'Forgive them, because they don't know what they're doing.'*

Was this a divine lie? So that the Father wouldn't come down to exterminate them, all he could do was justify them on the grounds of irresponsibility: 'They don't know.' In that hour he knew that even if these men had no clear idea of the enormity they were perpetrating, at any rate they knew how to hate and get drunk and sink into an orgy of vengeance. For that privilege they had given their children as hostages: '. . . *let his blood fall on our children.*'

How did they 'not know'? Weren't they aware that the curing of the blind, the raising of the dead, the marvellous stories he told from the boat to the poor deserved some other reward than this?

If it was a lie, it was the lie of a dying man. It was his last testament. And so the Father didn't open the earth to swallow them up, he didn't even touch a hair of a soldier's head. His final absolution or punishment was an enigma that remained hidden even from the Son. But on the little crowd busied around the cross the absurd clemency of heaven poured down in torrents. And the centurion who had spurred the executioners on would soon be struck like lightning with forgiveness to the point where he would cry out: '*This man really was the Son of God*'; and the mob who had flocked to enjoy the spectacle would go back home *beating their breasts* – they, too, seemingly bathed in the tidal wave of mercy.

Even on that very day, even at the third hour itself, the Father couldn't wreak vengeance. He'd been blackmailed by the Son who had presented him to those men not as the master of abysses and thunderbolts but as something much more grand and monstrous, as an enormous mouth of forgiveness.

With those few words he saved us – when he revealed to the Father and to us that we don't know what we're doing.

THE MIRACLE HE DIDN'T
WANT TO PERFORM

'*If you're the Son of God, come down from the cross . . .*'

To undo three nails would have been a mere trifle for a carpenter's son. In Joseph's workshop he had worked on wood up to the age of thirty, and there he still was, stuck between wood and nails. He could tell from the smell and texture whether this wood was beech, oak or chestnut. Three nails deeply wedged into the wood's white fibre – how many he had put in and pulled out! He knew how to do it. It would have been an easy miracle, scarcely a miracle at all.

The rabble shouted: 'Come down, impostor'; from up above he could see their mouths opening in blasphemies, their teeth gleaming in mockery and laughter. He could see the bronzed muscle-work of their shoulders, and the anxious heads of the soldiers bent over their dice. He could see his mother like a little black ant who, that evening, would remain alone on the pavements of the world.

Yes, he'd come down. By now everything had been fulfilled. He wouldn't take regrets to the Father. For the world to be redeemed the first tear shed in the garden was enough, the first drop of blood that spurted under the scourge. It would have been enough to say, 'this is what I want', without this strange journey into the prison of mankind, without taking on this flesh which was now one knot of pain. He had already emptied the cup; his body couldn't suffer any more because it was no longer a body; the last drop of blood had gone from it. And dying would be only too easy, it would add nothing to the sacrifice.

It would be a simple and quiet miracle. He would come down as from a ladder. The angels would immediately change the red holes of his wounds into roses and he would reach the ground unharmed. Having reached the ground he would go down the hill. They would go to Lazarus's house in Bethany. That very evening, in the gentle light of the two sisters, Mary would hear him telling wonderful things.

Yes, this was certainly the most necessary miracle if he wanted the world to believe in him. Get down. Nothing else would be needed, and thousands of martyrs would be spared ...

We would certainly have come down. Our mothers and our common sense would have torn us down with the nails still fixed in our hands and feet. We would have run away, trailing the hill with blood, towards the throne on to which terrified men who realized their mistake would finally raise us.

But he didn't want to work this miracle. The man on the cross knew that if he had done that, with the first contact of his feet with the ground all the other miracles told us in the gospel

197

would have been wiped out: the paralysed man would have lain down again on his pallet, the woman with the flow of blood would have begun to bleed again, the blind people of Jericho would have been plunged back again into darkness, the bodies of the ten lepers would have been racked with old sores, and Lazarus and the others would have disappeared for ever into the tombs he had emptied. Like fish in an immense sea that has unexpectedly dried up, men would have writhed convulsively about in a silent holocaust.

We can't understand. We'll never believe that life is bought with death and that this last breath from the breast is worth more than the gold of all the stars weighing on the night. But he who had made life and death and the stars knew it, and his parched mouth answered: 'No.'

TODAY

'Remember me, when you get to your kingdom.'

The thief hanging by his side was the only one who still believed that he was dying beside a king. For him, even though he couldn't read, that mocking inscription nailed above the cross – *Jesus of Nazareth, king of the Jews* – was truly a royal standard. The thief thought that his companion's kingdom would be a big garden with towers, fountains and fragrant wines. A paradise of open coffers where everything could be stolen with a clear conscience while you looked passers-by cheerfully in the eye because there'd be no guards. And the streets where he, as always, would sleep would be touched with the golden warmth of the sun and the night would know no winter. When he'd arrived up there, possibly in an ivory chariot, would the king be so kind as to remember him amid the bowing and scraping of his ministers?

Why should he *remember* him? What did *being remembered* mean to him? That highway robber was no sentimentalist. Did he perhaps mean that in the ditch where they would surely throw him graces and prayers might pour down on him? And what did grace and prayer mean? And then in what aspect would his friend remember him? As a bloodthirsty malefactor with his knife at his victim's throat and his hand on his purse? Or as he was now, hanging next to him, with his ugly blood-stained face and his great hairy belly? He didn't know and it didn't concern him. All he wanted was a little corner in Christ's memory – 'remember me'. If he'd had some little portrait he'd have shown it to him – as simple people do who strike up warm friendships on railway journeys.

The other thief was cursing, like the people down below. He was a furious blasphemer, but with a trace of cunning ('*If you're the Christ, save yourself and us*'). Perhaps – you never knew – if he abused that gentleman who had worked miracles, a miracle would result. Abuse – that was what was needed. And then the good thief rediscovered his violence (he'd have knifed him well and truly if his hands had been free) and addressed a last attack to his former accomplice: '*Aren't you even afraid of God, though you're undergoing the same punishment? It's only justice that we should suffer for our crimes, but he hasn't done any harm.*'

Yes, the one crucified between them was Christ. But the good thief didn't ask for a miracle, he didn't feel he had any right to be saved. He, who had lived on greed and robbery, was a crystal of total disinterestedness within himself.

Jesus answered: '*Today you'll be with me in paradise.*' The hardened evil-doer was accustomed to long years of waiting: five years condemned to the galleys, ten to the mines. But now those long periods were over. Jesus wasn't satisfied with wiping out all that man's stains. He hastened to assure him that immediately, today, he'd enter that garden without policemen where you sleep on warm streets.

'*Forgive them because they don't know what they're doing*', Christ asked. But the good thief could be absolved more easily: he knew what he was doing.

ANOTHER PARADISE

When he saw his mother . . .

He gave paradise to a dying man weighed down by crime. But when all's said and done, it's easy to give paradise to a heart that's stopping, to eyes that are closing. When the world wipes itself out and removes its claws from us, the soul that freely goes back to its dream is already paradise.

But the crucified man knew that even people who stay behind need a ghost of paradise. Men persist in looking for it here below. Our paradise is made up of faces: masks between us and the desert of time; smoke from the chimney of someone's fire, made for us; the warmth of a bed where another body is waiting; eyes, fingers, the words of every day.

The three Maries beneath the cross were useless now, they wouldn't be a bed or a fire for anyone. The same veil wrapped around them, the same name, the same weeping – they seemed a single destiny; but he knew that one of them spilt perfume on his feet in Simon's house; the other was Cleophas's wife, his mother's sister; and the third . . .

'Why were you looking for me? Didn't you know I had to go about my Father's business?' 'Woman, what does it matter to me or to you? My hour hasn't yet come.' 'I've no mother; my mother and my brothers are those who do the will of my Father.' 'I have come to set children against their mothers . . .' The story of the third woman was thick with these shafts, was one long steely blade in her heart, for Simeon in the temple couldn't have been wrong: *'. . . a sword will pierce your soul.'*

We'd have to go back in time to find the enchantment between that mother and that son, back to the starry night in Bethlehem when the shepherds and the simple women of the hillside thronged around her new-born child, or to the journey by donkey to Egypt when they were pressed together against the desert wind, or to the house at Nazareth when their happiness on certain evenings, and his serene way of looking

200

at her, made her hope that he'd renounce everything. But now we must return to the cross where Jesus was bleeding and looking at her.

And when Jesus saw his mother and next to her the disciple he loved, he said to his mother: 'Woman, here's your son.' Then he said to the disciple: 'Here's your mother.' The man on the cross knew that even the people who stay behind need a paradise; and ours is made up of faces: going on possessing, and calling and having ourselves called by the same name. From now on our paradise would be one of tears, because the real son was someone else and the mother was someone else too . . . different hair, different memories. Alas, if we could only play this comedy of adopted orphans, and when saying mother overcomes the jolt of nature.

But this applies to us who are still enclosed in the jealous shell of our bodies; we say 'friend' but aren't capable of *being* that friend, of mingling our mother with his, our child with his child. Christ's final lesson was against the heresy of blood-ties; in favour of identification with the friend, with each one of us; sudden reincarnation in the other, without too much anguish. In John, who took his place, he had already resurrected a little. His words were peremptory. He didn't say: 'Love him as a son; cherish her as a mother'; he said: 'Here's your son; here's your mother.' Just as, on the previous night, he didn't say: 'This bread symbolizes my body', but 'This bread is my body.'

And so from that moment there was no point in crying any more. *From that moment the disciple took her with him.*

THREE HOURS OF DARKNESS

It was the sixth hour, and a great darkness spread over all the land.

Why did it grow dark at this point? What had happened between heaven and earth? The scene was still the same, no one had thought up any new torture, the soldiers were still throwing dice for his tunic: the passion was stagnating in funereal expectation. But what was really happening was a death inside a death. During those three hours, until the ninth, he was wrestling with an even worse executioner, he was undergoing a more appalling annihilation. As in the garden, there was again this monstrous silence: but here it was a thousand times worse, because suddenly everything – his goodness and men's malice, the gentle cornfields and the polecats that laid them waste – all seemed utterly and grotesquely pointless.

As from the sixth hour the dying Christ was an orphan. He no longer had his mother, he'd given her to someone else. And now the Father died on him; those three hours of darkness were the agony of the Father in his brain.

'*My God, why have you abandoned me?*'

The other words that he said from the cross were forced out in a weak voice from an exhausted body. But these he shouted *with a great voice*; it was a shout which had to reach the most desperate and remote, those who would remain unmoved by the groans and the blood; all those who, when going over the story of the passion heard from a priest in their childhood, say: 'But my life is far worse than that afternoon on the cross.'

Within the layers of that darkness he was the God of those people. Where's the tragic pit in the depths of which man is most sad and most stifled by a deadly sickness? It's here: Christ plunged into it and was equal with all the unhappy people who have lost the Father; because he never reckoned to be born and to die among the living without sharing the ninth hour with us all.

'*Eli, lama sabachthani.*' He made himself our companion by identifying himself even with men's cry from the depths of despair – the cry that draws us all most closely together (like the prayer of the 'Our Father'): 'Why have you gone away?'

Eli, lama. These Aramaic syllables break down the doors behind which we've shut up God's orphans, those we call atheists: those whose greatness consists in shouting from their cross the same cry as Christ.

THE GLASS OF WATER YOU GIVE...

He said: 'I'm thirsty.' There was a bowl of vinegar there. The soldiers dipped a sponge into the vinegar and put it on the end of a hyssop stick and raised it to his lips.

Finally there was thirst. He'd climbed on to the gallows as dry as a snake. And as the blood flowed away thirst rose and took possession of him, it wrapped him round and shrivelled him up, so he drank with his cracked lips.

The yellow and dusty thirst of the desert; the ancient thirst of men and herds which spreads white bones over the heaths.

As long as there's some fluid one is still a man. The wounds and the nails can be endured. But when the last drop of water that keeps us humid has gone, then we're like burnt straw, we don't ask for life but for water.

So it was with him. '*I'm thirsty.*'

This was the first and last time he asked for any service. And they served him. For a moment hatred was suspended while they gave him something to drink; it was the truce of water, a thing so sacred that men can deprive a man of his blood but not of water for his thirst.

A little watered-down vinegar, a dark shining liquid rippling in the bowl . . . It seemed a mere trifle. But it was a little well of human pity that hadn't completely dried up.

The sponge against his lips was sweet indeed. For a few moments he got down from the cross and in the mad comfort of drinking he danced like a free child in the courtyards of Nazareth.

They had served him. It was a wooden stick that reached up to him. But down below, clasping the end, was a soldier's hand.

Christ slaked his thirst with that hand. And he chose this moment to die: when a hand was giving.

HANDS

'Into your hands I commend my spirit.'

So the Father was waiting for him. He had gone away and abandoned him, when he had to go away, and the Son was in the grip of black anguish. But now the Father returned, silently as before; his face was hidden, and perhaps behind the mystery he expressed neither alarm nor relief. But he held out his hands cupped in the shape of a shell. Only the Father can provide these hands for us to fall into.

Christ the Son merited forgiveness for our sin of despair: for that wild cry *'lama sabachthani'*. The Father had known that the last breath would make the rebel meek, that the final thought – no longer contaminated by things – would bring him back to him, as the moon brings back the sea over the rocks when the tide rises.

So then he held out his hands beneath Christ's mouth and they formed the mystical bowl of restitution. And Christ, *bowing his head, gave up his spirit.*

THE JOYFUL DEAD

Tombs opened and the bodies of holy people who had already gone to sleep rose again; and having come out of their tombs, after Jesus' resurrection they entered the city and appeared to many.

We needn't be frightened. We needn't look at the sanctuary veil rent from top to bottom, we needn't pay any attention to the earthquakes and rocks cleft in two.

In this scandal of disintegrating matter, of light and air dark with disgust at remaining with us men; at this ninth hour some people were happy, and these were the dead. The ghosts bending over behind the cemetery wall like young infantrymen all agog to leap from the trench for which they'd been drilled.

Their sleep had been an unquiet dream unconsciously ticking off the hours and the centuries. The dust into which their bodies had disintegrated was an hour-glass measuring the time – which had now struck – when they could burst out.

The captain was hanging on the hill. His terrified enemies – the living – ran away from that corpse without looking back. But the dead, the new masters, wandered along the roads of the countryside, went into gardens, spied through the windows of farmsteads – which the living quickly closed and barricaded themselves in – and knocked with their bones at the doors. For the dead had won. They hadn't risen again, it still wasn't permitted to resurrect before the captain. So they went around like skeletons. To sleep any more was unthinkable. They were undisciplined dead and triumphantly happy; impatient sentinels who, after their long freezing night on the ramparts, had profited by the first rays of dawn to observe that the enemy had raised the siege, and to go down into the city to greet their victory.

SHADOWS AND SCENTS

One of the soldiers pierced his side with a spear.

It was now the turn of the living to be ghosts. Until he had risen again. The actions they performed around the cross or at the most distant confines of the world were the actions of ghosts: soundless and bodiless illusions on a lime wall, which would vanish with the fading of the last light. The true body and reality was that white corpse; the true ruler of the world was that bloodless man, the motionless king who was frozen in the breath of the first stars and veiled by nocturnal dew.

The soldier who pierced his side and made the last drops of blood and water flow was a ghost; his spear was a ghost and so was his remorse. And down below were the ghosts of his friends *who stood in the distance watching these things*. In the distance. Soon they would turn their backs; cold as it was, a house was less cold than a dead man, so the city's smoking chimneys

205

would swallow up even Mary Magdalen, even Salome and James's mother – irresistibly. There was a period – we don't know how short or long it was – when the cross horrified everyone, no one could stay near it, and the empty space around it grew wider: all that remained to the crucified Christ was the company of the other two hanging from their crosses, as when a graveyard empties and the new arrival is left to join his own infinite silence to that of his neighbours.

Ghosts. But not only faces, not only sighs and sadness. In those flat phantoms there was the whole man, there was the best of him, the heart and the loving will to carry on. There was the ghost of Joseph, the old gentleman of Arimathaea, *who was one of his disciples but kept it quiet for fear of the Jews*. And he dared to call on Pilate *to ask permission to take away Jesus' body*. There was the ghost of Nicodemus, the one who had gone to visit him secretly, who now came forward with a hundred pounds of myrrh and aloes in payment for that nocturnal lesson . . . There was strength. Where did the ghosts find the strength to take the nails out of the cross, lift up that dead weight, lower it down the ladder and support it with so much robust tenderness? Joseph of Arimathaea (who did more than anyone else and may well have brought him down alone by entwining Christ's lifeless arm round his neck) found his strength in the secret joy that mingled with his tears – because Jesus was his, Pilate had given him to him when *he ordered that he should be given to Joseph*. And he, the good rich man, gave his new sepulchre in the nearby garden to Christ without a thought as to where he himself would go when he died: his white hands took charge of laying his friend in the cave, of wrapping him in the sheet he had bought for him, and of binding him in linens and spices.

Meanwhile other hands were working for Jesus. *Mary Magdalen, Mary the mother of James, Salome and the other women were standing at a distance to watch where they put him. Then they went home and prepared spices and perfumes.*

The passion of Christ was over. We can draw near, there's no more blood and nails. Now there are these ghosts and that strong scent that pervades everything.

RESURRECTION AND ASCENSION

Why are you looking among the dead for a man who's alive?

THE TWO LOVERS

When the sabbath was over, at the beginning of the first day of the week, there was a great earthquake.

CHRIST: Dying was frightful; but now being alive in death is unspeakable joy. The tomb is icy; and icy, too, were my mother to touch them, my chest and arms and legs. I feel growing inside me from hour to hour something like a snake that got folded within my limbs to prepare for its winter sleep. Is it possible to feel disgust at oneself and be as happy as I am? Yet my blood's drained away to the last drop. Touch me, if you're not scared to. Have you ever touched a fish on a fishmonger's slab, or thrown away a dead toad from outside the door? That cold thing wasn't flesh. And now I'm wholly that very thing.

DEATH: You're like all the other dead. I'm holding you tight in my embrace. You never wanted a woman, but now you're in my arms and you can't escape. No jealousy on my part is required to keep rivals off, because now I'm the only one who isn't repelled by you. I'll eat you up, every fibre of you, consume you entirely. Like all other dead people.

CHRIST: No, not really like other people. I'm different. I'm unspeakably happy here in the tomb. Peace? No, not that, not peace. The end of pain? No, not that either.

LIFE: Then what, my beloved? What enables you to be different from everyone else? And what's this happiness you're talking about now that death has torn you away from me?

CHRIST: Different from everyone else. I'm stiff as a puppet, it's true, like them. But I'm the last person who'll die. Today Death died with me on the cross.

DEATH: You're raving. I can't die, because being inside the dead is my very life.

LIFE: Don't listen to him, go on.

CHRIST: Death, I'm telling you, is dead. We've finished with Death, my friends. Alleluia.

Alleluia ... the hill of Bethlehem. You were happy on that hill, don't you remember? Shepherds and bagpipes ... Whereas nothing had yet happened then. You were all going to die. But today is Christmas. This darkness, this cold. This is the day of my gift to you. Soon. I'm waiting for the sign from my Father, because obedience to him is sweet. But meanwhile it's wonderful to talk in this darkness, to foretaste the miracle.

LIFE: Let's talk about it. You love me and are going to come back to me? Is that the miracle?

CHRIST: Yes. The miracle is just that. Whoever loves others as I loved them shall return to life after death.

LIFE: Others ... So isn't it me that you love? Isn't it for me that soon you'll come back to walk in the woods and bite into fragrant bread?

THE FIRST ANGEL OF THE TOMB: It's not for you, it's for them. He's dead, but what he feels for them is so strong that it'll put him on his feet again. It isn't your sensuous beauty, O Life; it isn't the Father that'll make him leap out of the darkness of the rock. It's because he can't stay in Death: Death is nothing but punishment for selfishness; the person who elects to live for himself alone is the one who remains in Death.

THE SECOND ANGEL OF THE TOMB: Christ risen from the dead, that prodigy which people will wonder at or laugh at for thousands of years, is only the great leap into freedom.

LIFE: But how can he do that if he's dead?

A POET: But we too are certain of not dying. Why else should we be happy on certain days, and dance and laugh?

We know only Life and we love it very much. And each of us says to himself: Is it possible that Death can be overcome?

Those two old men on the bench have no future to look

forward to, yet they're serene and gesticulate as if they were going to a better tomorrow. Listen to them – they're talking about places they used to know and of days gone by that will return.

The woman beating out her rags against her garret railing is singing.

The man with cancer of the throat is enjoying his ice-cream.

The mother has taken a chair to the graveyard and is sewing a little garment beside the grave of her child.

Addicts are injecting their arms with a drug to free themselves from Death and are already in the painted ecstasy of the resurrection.

The falling mountaineer doesn't think for a second that this is the last time he'll see the golden peaks where he lost his life.

DEATH: But everyone will go on dying. When their heart stops beating, I shall be their master and destroy them, I'll even make their memories decay.

LIFE: That's how it would be if he hadn't passed through these three days, in your cold arms, and if he weren't soon going to leave you in humiliation on the ground . . .

DEATH: There's a heavy stone closing this inn of mine.

LIFE: Here comes the earthquake. What a quiet earthquake, and yet it's the most mighty one that has ever taken place! It isn't producing any rumble or shock. It's all in his heart which has started beating again. And the large stone is obediently rolling from the entrance, it's drawing back like a good giant.

CHRIST: I'm going out into the light, for this is the dawn of Easter. Joseph's garden is bright with dew beneath my feet. The eastern sky is tinged with blood. What currency blood is! It alone buys. I'm buying everyone. I'm buying sorrow and pain, blasphemy and perdition. On Calvary hill I spat out the sponge dipped in vinegar, but now I'm swallowing Death so that it won't go on sprouting. It will be the final horror of my passion. And then music, music until the end of the world.

WHY TO ME?

MARY MAGDALEN: It's always as if it was yesterday, isn't it, Salome? And yet twenty years have passed. Or a thousand, I don't know.

SALOME: I feel like that too, Mary. And every time I meet you, like today, I have to make you tell me yet again what happened that morning, so as to be sure I didn't dream it.

MARY: It wasn't a dream. But all the rest of my life before then was a dream, and a dream that fills me with horror, always spent in the arms of different men who seemed like corpses. But when I washed his feet I woke up, and I've been awake ever since. And ever since that night they nailed him to the cross and we prepared our ointments for him, I've never slept. That's why I look so old.

SALOME: We all grew old that night. Those ointments we prepared to embalm him with had more tears in them than myrrh and aloes.

MARY: And the dawn of that morning – you remember? That dawn – it began in anguish, at least for me.

SALOME: Off we all went, quickly, when it was still almost dark, clutching our jars of perfume under our shawls. You were the most distressed; you didn't say a word.

MARY: You went on asking: 'Who'll roll back the stone from the entrance?' I ran ahead, and the stone had already been rolled back. It was like dying. Not even his body was on the earth any more, and all our work during the night was for nothing. I was a coward. I didn't dare go in to prove that the tomb was empty. I left you without a word. And I ran and ran to find Peter and John so as to get some sort of news from his friends that was different, some comforting explanation. And I shouted at them, though I could hardly breathe: *'They've taken the Lord away from the tomb . . .'*

SALOME: Whereas we went in, and there were two people sitting there wearing beautiful clothes. One talked to us. He said: *'Why are you looking among the dead for a man who's alive?'*

And he said other marvellous things, but I couldn't hear them or understand them and I don't think the others could either. We were too frightened and too happy. We made our escape and our only care was not to break our jars. And we didn't say anything to anyone.

MARY: I saw you coming out. I was weeping there outside. When I saw you fleeing like that I imagined the worst. The two you mentioned asked me: *'Woman, why are you crying?'* And when I turned to answer, someone else was there. And he too asked me: *'Why are you crying? Who are you looking for?'* I thought he was the gardener; so I appealed to him with anger: *'If it's you who've taken him away, tell me where you've put him, and I'll find him.'* How could I not have recognized him? That's my great regret that I'll have all my life. I ill-treated him, perhaps I hated him for an instant . . .

SALOME: You couldn't have recognized him – it was still dark and your eyes were swollen with crying and you'd been up all night preparing those ointments.

MARY: Then he said, *'Mary'*, and he'd only risen again at that moment, so that it seemed as if he'd risen for me alone. At least that's what I was sure of and I didn't think of the others. And there go more regrets.

SALOME: Not for you alone, Mary. Of course you were the first to see him and that's what he wanted, he made that choice. He chose you.

MARY: Why did he choose me, the whore from Magdala? Instead of his mother, or John?

SALOME: Don't ask why. And what happened then? Tell me, because it's always good for us to live those moments again.

MARY: Then, though I was frozen to a stone, he read my thoughts and knew I was going to throw myself into his arms, so he said: *'Don't touch me.'*

SALOME: He came up to us and said, *'Don't be afraid; tell my brothers to go to Galilee and they'll see me there.'*

MARY: But he let you touch him. You gathered round his feet and embraced them as I'd done that day at Simon's banquet . . . But that was quite right. You were good, you were wives and mothers. Whereas I . . .

SALOME: That had nothing to do with it, Mary. Don't torment yourself. It wasn't because of that. Anyway, you were given the first fruits of the joy – what could you ask more?

MARY: But why to me – why?

SALOME: Too many things are mysterious.

MARY: Yes. Even when I hurried to his friends and told them Jesus was alive and that I'd seen him they didn't believe me. That's mysterious too.

SALOME: And it's mysterious that the whole thing should be so bright in our memories after so many years, just as if it was yesterday.

THE RACE

But the other disciple was more agile than Peter and arrived first at the tomb.

JOHN: Hold me under my elbows, my dear brothers, and help a very old man to drag one foot behind the other. You love me and venerate me because I talked to him and touched him; I'm the last survivor of those who were alive with him. I'm nearly a hundred and once Peter thought, when he heard one of the Master's phrases, that I'd never die; but I shall die.

You venerate what I say and even more my hoary head because one night I heard the beating of Christ's heart. That's why you often put your arms round me and kiss me. But when I drag myself around like this I make you feel pity, you'd never think that once I was young and quick and on that sabbath morning beat Peter in the race to the tomb. Yes, I did beat him. I was younger than him. But that's why I stopped at the entrance where the stone had been rolled away. Just because Peter was now our leader. It would have been insolent to go in before him without waiting; it would have been against the charity our master had taught us. I just glanced inside; all I could see were the linen bands on the ground, nothing else.

Peter arrived a moment later (though to me it seemed a century), all panting and breathless. I let him go in first. I already *believed*, though I couldn't check things much. But I wanted my friend to be ahead of me even in believing. One reason was because his nature was ... well, I wouldn't say sceptical, but headstrong. He was distrustful and found loyalty hard.

In we went. Besides the linen bands that I'd already seen from outside, there was also the shroud – *not among the bands but folded up and laid on one side.* Then I could only think of myself, and enjoy the truth that he'd risen again, the conviction I'd had when I was running and even before I started to run. But my conviction was like a bird in flight that didn't know where to perch. Enjoying joy.

Because of my reverence for my elder which made me wait that instant (it was the biggest sacrifice of my life) you now hold me up with filial love, you carry me through the streets, you take the place of my poor feeble legs. But these legs – you'll enjoy knowing it and laughing with me – once beat Peter at running.

WE DON'T BELIEVE IT

While they were arguing and discussing together, Jesus himself joined them and walked along with them.

CLEOPAS'S COMPANION: Listen, brothers: Cleopas and I were on our way to Emmaus and were arguing and discussing. Then the Lord came and joined us and said: '*Why are you so sad?*'

CLEOPAS: I said, '*Are you such a stranger in Jerusalem that you don't know about all these recent goings-on?*' And we told him what had happened, about the crucifixion, and about the rumours going around, among women and angels, that Jesus was still alive.

THE COMPANION: Then he began talking, and talked for the whole of the rest of the journey. Do you remember, Cleopas? He said some hard things. He rebuked our scepticism. '*Your hearts are too dull and reactionary to believe all the prophets said...*'

CLEOPAS: Yes, some things were hard. But his voice was the very opposite – so warm and full of mercy that I didn't feel a pin-prick from what he said, nor any remorse.

THE COMPANION: It was like that with me too. Do you remember when he embarked on that difficult subject of scripture and prophecy? I hardly understand anything of sciences like that – I feel bored when the masters of law talk about them. But from his lips those things could have gone on for ever as far as I was concerned.

CLEOPAS: But unfortunately the road didn't go on for ever. Nor did the day. If only the moon could have stayed where it was and not climb up over the rooftops! I've often been to Emmaus, but I'd never noticed before in any village in Galilee such sweetness and awe as the evening brings there. In Emmaus it seems that it can't be any other hour than the one when the inns are lighting up on the road and the birds going to sleep in the leaves.

THE COMPANION: So we said to him: '*Stay with us here because it's evening already and the sun is setting.*'

CLEOPAS: When we sat down at table, before we ate, he took the bread, blessed it, and offered it to us.

THE COMPANION: It seemed as if first his hands, and then the whole of him, entered into that bread as if by magic. In a few seconds he had vanished from our sight and only the bread remained.

CLEOPAS: So we recognized him when it was too late, and meanwhile darkness had fallen outside.

THE COMPANION: But if you think it over, Cleopas, we'd experienced something, something extraordinary, even before that. *Weren't our hearts burning in our breasts while he was talking to us along the road?*

AN APOSTLE: Brothers, the Lord has really risen and has appeared to Simon.

CLEOPAS: And to us too, as we've described to you. At Emmaus, when evening was falling.

THE BROTHERS: We don't believe it.

TOUCHING, EATING

Because of their joy they found it hard to believe . . .

They didn't believe because of their joy. People don't believe in joy. So Jesus patiently went in through the bolted door of the house where they were eating and approached with his palms outstretched: *'Look at my hands and my feet; it's really me. Touch, and you'll be convinced . . .'* And he uncovered his side and offered them his fifth wound.

But *they found it hard to believe and were amazed.* So Jesus patiently asked them: *'Have you anything to eat?'* And they brought him roast fish and honeycombs, scrutinizing his mouth as he chewed, and his throat as he swallowed the food they'd just been savouring themselves. They stared, and no one spoke.

On coming in he'd wished peace on them all, but in their turmoil of joy and fear and scepticism their hearts were anything but peaceful. Then Jesus patiently rebuked them for not believing, so they became a little happier and a little nearer to peace. Because a ghost wouldn't rebuke them with so much love. Because finally he had breathed on their faces, and a new, wild and potent emotion had entered into them.

THE FINGER

But Thomas wasn't there with the others when Jesus came.

Jesus had patiently noted that one of them was missing on the day of the fish and the honeycomb; one who, returning home, said: *'Unless I see the holes made by the nails in his hands and put my finger in the nail-wounds and my hand in his side, I shan't believe.'*

So he came back to look for that one. *'Put your finger here in my side . . .'*

That unbelieving finger revived the pain of that wound – it was more painful than the soldier's spear on that now distant day.

'*My Lord and my God*', said the finger.

'*You believe, Thomas, because you've seen,*' said Jesus; '*blessed are those who haven't seen and yet believe.*'

Perhaps we shall be saved through that wound which seeks us out at home and patiently shows itself. But we won't ever be blessed. We'll just be fools with a finger in a wound and eyes lowered in shame.

THE LAST PICNIC

At break of day Jesus appeared on the shore; but the disciples didn't know that he was Jesus.

On that day too, by the lake of Tiberias, Jesus took food to tame these frightened and suspicious animals. In each of these encounters we find him anxious to use the concrete fact of food to diminish a spirituality too magical for them to endure it.

'*Haven't you got something to eat, my sons?*' The men on the boat didn't yet know who he was. Possibly a beggar, or a friend with an appetite. They weren't in a cordial mood. In the depths of their hearts they had the happiness of knowing that he was alive; they had met him and enjoyed his company twice. But this wasn't a good day: they'd spent the whole night fishing, because they had to eat every day, and hadn't caught a thing. They'd picked up the thread of their life again, between fishnets and long discussions at table in the evening – their life with its light and shade of good and bad luck.

'*No*', they answered.

But as soon as they followed the advice of that man on the shore, and cast their nets to the right, they got an enormous catch; so that John, always the infallible sentinel of love, cried out: '*It's the Lord.*' It was him, there could be no mistake about it: if good things happened, it was a sign of him. Then Peter plunged headlong into the water. He hardly had time to remember he was naked and to tie his clothes round him.

The wild joy – John's outburst and Peter's leap – because they were in the boat. But when they were on shore and met

216

his eyes, and his voice was near, saying: '*Bring the fish here, come and eat . . .*', then there was that senseless timidity and awkward silence again. They knew it was him, everyone's heart was pounding, and they had a thousand things to say to him; *but no one dared to ask him:* '*Who are you?*'

Jesus helped them. He distributed the bread and the fish he'd already prepared on a fire he'd kindled. He knew that they liked things better that way, chewing and gazing at him, rather than speaking.

THE ALPHABET

For the third time he asked him . . .

After their silent meal it was again Jesus who broke the silence. It was a question without preamble, like a stone thrown at one's head, utterly straightforward and all the more disconcerting: '*Simon, son of John, do you love me more than the others do?*'

Only the Man no longer subject to this life and its discretions could ask a question like that: and ask it in front of everyone in incautious head-on terms. He wanted to know whether Peter loved him, and loved him more than James and Matthew and Philip and Bartholomew, more even than John.

Was Peter happy? Why did he have to be snatched from his reserve in this way? Why was he required to play with words, and why wasn't the Master – who could read people's hearts – content this time too to find the answer himself in the depths of Peter's rustic thoughts? He swallowed his saliva, recapitulated the story between him and his extraordinary friend from the day of the big haul when he and Andrew joined up with Jesus ('*Follow me, and I'll make you fishers of men*'), to the day of the high praise ('*You're blessed, Simon . . . and I'll give to you the keys of the kingdom of heaven*') – and then those thousand days and nights spent with him, the miracles, the dead opening their eyes, the outbursts against his arrogance, Christ's head bent to wash his feet, and his bitter lament that selfsame night – '*Are*

217

you asleep, Simon? Couldn't you have watched with me for an hour?' –
and again on that night the crowing of the cock . . .

Peter wasn't happy: he would have liked to weep and he
couldn't, to answer and he didn't know how, to throw that
sackful of memories of sun and tears at Christ's feet and run
away . . . But Jesus was silently waiting.

'Yes, Lord, you know I love you.'

He had to say it three times, because the Master repeated his
absurd question three times as though he were deaf or absent-
minded. On the third occasion the fisherman, disheartened and
impatient, extricated himself by appealing to his interlocutor's
powers: *'You know everything, you know I love you.'*

He didn't know everything. This at any rate was something
that he didn't want to know through his own means alone. In
that strange, solemn and childish question that so disconcerted
Peter and his companions lay the whole alphabet of those three
years, the whole meaning of his journey, perdition or salvation.
He had risen again and delayed another forty days on earth to
hear himself answered, and to answer 'I love you', so as to
ascend with this certainty into glory which otherwise wouldn't
have been glory.

And what then? What followed if Peter loved him? What
could he do with the love of a stubborn, cowardly and talkative
man? Perhaps in his heart Peter imagined he might finally have
to opt for some gentle form of communal life, as between
friends on whose goodness one can count. His proposal on
Mount Tabor – 'Lord, let's set up three tents here' – had come
to nothing; but a tent would still be possible in some recess
among the rocks. With the other companions too, if he wanted
them – because they also loved him. Or just in a fishing-
boat, where they could sleep at night and cook fish in the evening.

But Christ had decided otherwise. *'Feed my sheep'*, he said.
'Feed my lambs, feed my sheep.'

'Your lambs, your sheep? Who are they, how many, and
where? And what does it involve?' Yes, of course – Peter
certainly understood in a vague kind of way: the others, his
brothers. He would feed them: if this was the sign of loving

218

him, if the two things – as that voice seemed to imply – were one and the same.

Then Peter was happy. He had satisfied the Lord. He would watch not just for an hour (as he hadn't been able to do in the garden) but for many, many nights, for his whole life he would watch over his friend's sheep. And he hoped his life would be long.

But what was the sense of these other words Jesus was adding: '... *when you're old you'll offer your hands and someone else will bind you and take you where you don't want to go*'? He saw a white sea of lambs, he felt the wool between his fingers, he heard the bleating. But he didn't hear the hammer-blows, he didn't see them leading an old fisherman to another cross, and nailing him on it upside down.

DON'T LOOK UP AT THE SKY

And while he was blessing them, he left them and was taken into the sky in their presence.

Surely the sky is the loveliest thing the Father created, because we can possess it and be possessed by it without touching it. It's an object that arouses no lust, a land where no brawls break out nor taverns ferment. It's heaven. In the first stages, when I'd only just left the ground, butterflies and ladybirds brushed past me; then the last of these tiny lives, dragonflies, followed me in a more soaring flight. Then further above there were the geometrical darts and swoops of the swallows, and the last sentinels of the air, the falcons. Then no more life, or rather the life of the clouds that fold over in secret winds or spread out in lazy shapes such as swans or bagpipes or huge hares whose ears extend to make a sailing-boat. Yet further up the sky is no more than precious transparency, the blue jewel that dawn will change into pearl, and sunset to pink, the very stuff of the soul and freedom. Here lies condensed the enchanted emotion of all exoduses, the liberation from all slaveries, the human destiny of sailing away from a sorrow that we leave behind us (that will become a good poem or a legend) towards that happiness which always lies in morning departures.

And on I sail in this happy silence, having no other port but silence.

I rise up but as I rise I won't stop talking to you, because it's only if you hear the things I'm saying that this hour will be bearable for you. Seen from down there – among gardens and houses that grow smaller and smaller – this hour is infinitely sad, this day that all calendars call the Ascension is for you the end of a long Christmas, and among these fleecy clouds that happy night on which I came down among you fades utterly away. A crib meant making a barrier, barriers, basket-work around me on a feast-day that coincided with your childhood, with the happiness of your fireplaces. But where are they now, and what was the use of all your cribs?

This hour may seem even sadder to you than the hour of my death. The cross still left you my body to anoint with tears and perfumes, to visit with flowers and lanterns. I know that for you a tomb on earth can be more comforting than an unreachable point in heaven.

But if with a leap I abandon the earth at the very height of my youth and victory, in the sun of my friendships and my suppers, it is to tell you that you, too, haven't got your home down below: Bethany and its stone dog, its doorposts decorated with ears of corn – today I'm teaching you to leave them without looking back. Your home isn't there even when in the body.

This body which seems made for the earth, look how I tear it away like a reconquered flag, and lift myself with it up there, towards the real homeland.

I know you find it difficult to understand. All you understand is that I was down below among you and now I'm not there any more; that you could touch me and now all that remains of me on earth are my footsteps soon to be swept away by the wind. You would have preferred a god who remained fixed in your furrows, even a stone god like the ancient idols, whose forehead you could stain with wine at the time of the grape-harvest, a

god round whom you could dance and on whom moss and ivy,
rain and snow would mark the changes in your seasons.

I rise upwards and defeat the earth and your psychology as
wingless animals. The hard part of your life is now beginning.
But I foresaw it, I told you (persistently don't you remember?):
'*A little while more and you'll see me again ... I won't leave you
orphans ... I'll stay with you until the consummation of the ages ...
I'm going to the Father but I'll come back ... I'll send you the Spirit
and your sadness will be turned into joy.*' But all the same the hilltop
green with olive trees where you're now gathered seems to you
a last tip of rock for the shipwrecked and abandoned; and when
I see your beards all tilted upwards, your black forelocks and
bald heads that will tumble down like a heap of puppets when
the show's over, my heart is troubled by an absurd remorse.
Forgive me this vertical flight from the hill. I'm taking with me
your sadness at Emmaus, the twilight round the table in the
inn, and Cleopas's imploring voice: 'Evening is coming, stay
with us.'

When the clouds have hidden me from your eyes, you'll go
on gazing at their restlessly shifting shapes against the silk of
heaven. You'd like to stay there for thousands of years, because
you were told *he'll come back exactly as you saw him rise*. Then
two men dressed in white will tell you to go home. Obey them, go
down with the others. And when you've shut your door behind
you, and stand among your poor possessions, and then lean out
of your window, know that I have still another thing to tell
you. Don't look up at the sky. On this day of the Ascension
I'm hiding behind a cloud, but I could equally hide myself
behind a bush, in the hollow trunk of a tree or in a pool in
Galilee. The Father to whom I'm going doesn't live beyond the
flight of birds. He's on the moors swept by the wind, in
unknown haystacks where you may happen to sleep one night,
on mountain ridges, under the bed, and on the roofs of cities.

After I've ascended, he and I will be wherever you are in the
world. Then nothing will be strange to you. Whenever you set
foot in a strange land you'll recognize it behind some hidden
memory because I shall have lived there for you. Whenever you
leave a country you'll know that you're not altogether

abandoning it, because you'll leave me there. Everywhere will become your motherland and your home. Distances will be wiped out from the moment when I left the hilltop and set out on my travels through the world. Then you'll understand that I only pretended to go away. You'll understand it for this reason: that you'll no longer feel afraid.

My life doesn't end here; if it ended you too would die. It goes on even when you wish for dissolution, because it's precisely in me that you long to be dissolved. Every despair, every travail of your day is a desire to reunite yourselves with me, to see me again on the clouds, to serve me at table.